A KAYAK FULL *of* GHOSTS

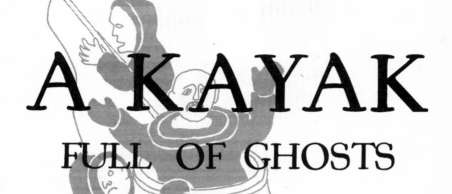

A KAYAK
FULL OF GHOSTS

ESKIMO TALES
GATHERED AND RETOLD BY
LAWRENCE MILLMAN

Illustrated by Timothy White

CAPRA PRESS
SANTA BARBARA

Some of these stories have appeared in
*Sulfur, Cultural Survival Quarterly, Shaman's Drum,
Mid-American Review, Short Story International,*
Zyzzyva, and *Nantucket Review.*

Cover design by Judy Sutcliffe
Illustrations by Timothy White
Design and typography by Jim Cook
SANTA BARBARA, CALIFORNIA

LIBRARY OF CONGRESS CATALOGING IN PUBLICATION DATA
A Kayak full of ghosts.
1. Eskimos—Legends   2. Eskimos—Greenland—Legends.
3. Indians of North America—Legends.   I. Millman, Lawrence
E99.E7K27   1987   398.2'08997   87-11729
ISBN 0-88496-267-9 (PBK)

Published by
CAPRA PRESS
Post Office Box 2068
Santa Barbara, California 93120

Contents

I. ORIGINS AND ANCESTORS

The Woman of the Sea / 19
Sun and Moon / 21
The Origin of Daylight / 22
The Louse and the Worm / 23
The Birth of Fog / 24
The Thunder Children / 26
The Girl Who Married Her
    Dog / 28
Sila, the Weather Spirit / 30
The Origin of Women / 31
The Origin of Wind / 33

The Pleiades / 34
The First Narwhal / 36
The Father of Fish / 38
Mosquitoes / 39
The Origin of Sharks / 40
The First Walrus / 41
Flies / 42
Of Giants and Human
    Beings / 43
Killing People Is Wrong / 44

II. CHILDREN

Kakuarshuk / 47
The Northern Lights
    Children / 49
The Child Who Lived In All
    Things / 50
The Unwanted Child / 52
The Boy Who Was Raised By
    Foxes / 53
Ussarqak, Who Ate Too Many
    Heads / 55

Qituarssuk / 56
Arviaq and the Worm / 57
Qalaganguase, Who Had No
    Strength / 58
The Spoon Monster / 60
Tulugaq, Who Was Barren / 61
The Monstrous Child / 63
Anarteq / 64

III. MAGIC AND TABOOS

"The Earth Will Know" / 69
Every Taboo Is Holy / 70
The Sick Raven / 71
The House of Reindeer / 72
The Cure / 74
Katerparsuk, the Orphan / 75
Bad Food / 77
The Rival Angakoks / 78
The Spirit of the Shit-Pile / 79
The Entrail Thief / 80
Him-Whose-Penis-Stretches-
    Down-To-His-Knees / 81

"I Am Only Shit" / 82
The Brother-in-Law Who
    Became a Bear / 83
A Tale of Motherlove / 84
The Feasting of House
    Ghost / 86
Don't Forget to Pray / 87
Niarqoq / 88
Namik / 89
The Lame Man's Stick / 90
Erdlaversissoq / 92

IV. HUMAN BEINGS

The Glutton / 95
Imarasugssuaq / 96
The Fox-Wife and the Penis of the
    Lake / 98
Blubber Boy / 100

Uutaaq, the Hunter / 102
Counting Hairs / 103
Utsuuq / 104
The Sisters Who Married
    Erqigdlit / 106

(IV. HUMAN BEINGS, cont'd.)

The Ghost That Ate Children / 109
Evat / 111
The Two Women Who Found
Freedom / 112
Konjujuk's Friend / 114
Terqilik and His Sons / 116
Katiak / 117
Oherdluq, the Murderer / 119
Pavia, Who Made Friends With a
Stone / 121
Arnatsiq / 123
The Jealous Husband / 124
Girl of Stone / 126
The Woman Who Married Her
Son's Wife / 127

Tugtutsiak / 129
The Man Who Was a
Mother / 130
Four Wives / 131
Nutik / 133
Mikisoq and the Skull / 134
The Luckless Hunter / 135
Nakasungnak, the Fool / 137
Two Men, One Kayak / 139
Sermerssuaq / 140
The Iron-Tailed Woman / 141
Asalok's Family / 143
Island of Women / 145
The Slab of Meat / 146

V. ANIMALS

The Raven and the Seagull / 149
Whale's Wife / 150
The Mother's Skull / 151
"Spare My Life" / 153
The Raven and The Whale / 154
The Two Girls and Their
Husbands / 156
Inugarssuk / 158
The Giant Eider Duck / 159
The She-Bear / 161
The Wife Who Turned Into a
Raven / 163

The Raven and the
Hunter / 164
"Am I Not a Handsome
Brute?" / 165
The Greedy Eagle / 167
The Eider Duck's
Revenge / 168
Guillemots / 169
The Lustful Raven / 171
Tiggak / 173

VI. DEATH AND OLD AGE

The Collector of Ravens / 177
Meqqoq and the Stone People / 178
The Magic Bear / 180
The Kayaker Who Flew / 182
The Old Woman Who Was Kind
to Insects / 184
Natatoq, the Storyteller / 185
The Hole in the Cliffs / 188
The Old Man Who Ate His
Grandson / 189
Umaq, Who Danced / 190
Tuglik and Her Grand-
daughter / 191

Old Age / 192
The Old Seal-Hunter from
Aluk / 193
"I Have Sent Them My
Death..." / 195
The Man and His Wife Who
Raised the Dead / 196
Skeletons / 198
Kivioq, Whose Kayak Was Full
of Ghosts / 199
What is the Earth? / 201

Glossary / 202

Sources of the Tales / 203

"All true wisdom is only to be found far from the dwellings of men, in the great solitudes; and it can only be attained through suffering. Suffering and privation are the only things that can open the mind of man to that which is hidden from his fellows."

Igjugarjuk of the Caribou Eskimos,
to Knud Rasmussen

INTRODUCTION

THE EAST GREENLAND VILLAGE of Kulusuk sits on an island as bare as an old golf ball. No trees, shrubs, or vegetable gardens grace its windswept geology. The soil is so sparse that the bodies of the dead are simply covered up with rocks; and a prayer is offered to the Almighty that He keep a close watch over the departed so that they won't end up as the main course in a sled dog's supper.

In November 1980, I flew to Kulusuk with a bush pilot of my acquaintance, an Icelander named Helgi. Helgi had an Eskimo girlfriend there. Never mind that she was a drunken, knife-wielding termagant. Helgi loved her. And his love for her gave me a splendid opportunity to explore a village unvisited by whites until 1884 when Captain Gustav Holm of the Danish Navy came in search of the lost Norse colony. I photographed the burial cairns, the Carlsberg lager cairns, the corrugated iron houses, and a man carving a *tupilak* from a polar bear's thigh bone. Then, as I backed up to get a panoramic view of the village, I lost my footing. Down I slipped, down an icy incline and through a coating of ice and into the fjord. Whereupon I blacked out. Next thing I knew, I was lying in the Kulusuk infirmary, shivering furiously. The resident nurse, trained in Copenhagen, couldn't control my shivering. Helgi gave me a bone-crunching Icelandic massage, but that didn't help the shivering either. Nor was it helped by the Greenlandic children who arrived to giggle at me. Then an old toothless

9

woman came in and began rubbing a sticky substance into my skin. Walrus fat? Seal oil? No, it was Crisco and she said that she always used it on her sons whenever they seemed to be suffering from over-exposure. For Crisco shut in body warmth even as it shut out the cold, sealing up the pores of the skin. And in a very short time, I stopped shivering altogether. Now I could drink a cup of tea without spilling its contents. Crisco had triumphed.

But the wrong step turned out to be precisely the right step. I was sharing the infirmary with an ancient-looking man of about fifty who had been celebrating a bit too much the night before and was now in for a dry out. As most Greenlanders have Danish names, this man's name was Gustav. He was a seal hunter. I told him my story about falling into the fjord, which he found vastly amusing (*"Tipi, tipi,"* he laughed). In fact, he found it so amusing that he started telling me stories of his own, less amusing, about the *tunumiut* ("people of the backside," or so the relatively few Eastlanders are called by West Greenlanders). I heard about a local woman named Keligasak who ate three generations of her own family during the terrible famine years of the last century, when winters were stuck together, in the Greenlandic phrase, "like copulating dogs." I heard tales about blood feuds that made the Hatfields and McCoys sound like Amos and Andy. I heard about an ancestor of Gustav's whose hobby was mass murder; not so impractical a hobby as it might seem when one remembers that, according to East Greenland custom, a murderer is entitled to all the game that his victim would have killed if he had remained alive.

Such stories were a pleasure and a revelation to me. From the same tradition I had known only versions watered-down for the benefit of polite Anglo children. Gustav's stories had guts; they were brutal, scatological, weirdly comic, and moral—rather, I thought, like much contemporary fiction. I stayed in Kulusuk a few more days and heard more of Gustav's stories. Likewise, I heard a few stories from the *tupilak* carver, who was a cousin of Georg Uparsima, the last man in Greenland to get his training as an *angakok* (shaman). Since Georg had died in the 1970s, no one was able to make the drum dance all by itself. Old Georg could. He could see the vapor arising from the impurity of a menstruating woman. The *tupilak* carver told me one of Georg's own stories about a fellow *angakok* who could pull off his genitals and stick them back on again, no problem. When at last I left Kulusuk, I did so with something like a resolve to wander the North in search of stories. Perhaps I associated them with getting well again.

A year or so later, I was sitting in a tent in Auyittuq National Park on Baffin Island. My companion was an Eskimo storyteller from Pangnirtung named Ken Annanack. For several days, heavy rains and a howling autumn gale had been lashing our tent in a series of nasty two-part improvisations. We were prisoners of the weather and had little else to do but eat chunks of seal meat and cauterize our intestines with cup after cup of strong black coffee. At first the talk had been somewhat desultory, touching on hockey, women, and the virtues of .22 rimfires. But when Ken started to tell stories, his voice took on a new intensity. It was as if he had suddenly sat down on our Primus stove. He told me about a man who tried to eat the weather. I heard about a man who was transformed into a salmon and an entire group of men transformed into bears. He brought up the subject of cannibalism. "Around 1900," he said, "my grandfather had to eat a little child to keep from starving. The child was going to die anyway. My grandfather said that it tasted like inferior bear meat." We stopped to brew more coffee. The wind howled. And into the teeth of this wind more stories were hurled; long untold stories; half forgotten stories; mere local anecdotes *(oqalualat);* and even a few larger myths *(oqalugtuat).* I remember thinking that this was how stories ought to be told—during riproaring weather, over an abundance of meat, surrounded by a sawtooth of crags and Ice Age glaciers. And not, I hasten to say, during the so-called "poetry reading" undergone in the parlors of academe, which by comparison seems like so much polishing of mahogany.

Actually, my experience in the tent was not dissimilar to a

classic Eskimo storytelling session. Once upon a time stories were
narrated during or directly after huge banquets of frozen raw
meat. These banquets took place in a communal feasting house
called a *qagshé*. The point was to force as much meat down one's
throat in as short a time as possible. A healthy man would have
no difficulty eating twenty-five pounds of raw meat in half a day; a
tribute not so much to exuberance as to a feast-or-famine mental-
ity. However, the less food is broken up by chewing, the sooner it
reaches the belly; the sooner it reaches the belly, the longer it
takes to digest; and the longer it takes to digest, the more food
value can be extracted from it.

Thus, the storyteller becomes both an aid to digestion and, in a
curious way, a source of protein. For this age-old ritual of gluttony
may have created a primal link in the Eskimo mind between
sustenance and stories. Words=food= life. *Akiortopah. My belly is
content. So, too, is my spirit.*

But today's banquet is tomorrow's pangs of hunger. It is not
surprising that the main theme of Eskimo tales is the desperate
search for food. No landscape is more frugal with its gifts than the
North. Sometimes a crust of ice scarcely thicker than the one I fell
through has meant the difference between starvation and well
being. Yet in no other landscape has so much been utilized for
survival. Eskimos have proved themselves capable of eating just
about anything, including each other. Seal eyes and reindeer marrow they still consider the choicest of delicacies and the green
fermented jucies of a walrus's stomach the most piquant of sea-
sonings. The slime from a walrus hide, garnished with human
urine, was once thought to be princely fare. And then there was a
time when a woman would take a mouthful of blubber, chew it,
spit it out, take another mouthful, chew it and spit it out, until she
had spat out a puddle deep enough to steep angelica stalks—such
was dessert in the old days. Even today the Eskimo displays very
little gustatory qualm. Near Fort Chimo, Quebec, I was offered a
snack of, I thought, crowberries. One taste told me the truth. They
weren't crowberries, but caribou droppings cooked in seal fat. I

declined any more. The man who offered them to me shrugged and continued to pop them into his mouth like salted peanuts.

I gathered my stories from Northwest Territories, Baffin Island, northern Quebec, Labrador, and both coasts of Greenland. I gathered them from hunters, fishermen, garage mechanics, airline stewardesses, and not a few ranking officers in the army of the unemployed and unemployable. From a man waiting for a bus in Nuuq, Greenland, I captured several tales. Occasionally I found myself in a drinking place next to a person who turned out to be a first-rate teller of tales. Chance is the mother of invention. Invention is also the mother of invention. As a man in Nain, Labrador, told me: "A story is not true unless the storyteller puts something of his own in it."

My task was never, ever easy. First of all, there was the fact that I'm a *qallunaaq,* a White Man: mightn't my eagerness for stories be yet another sort of white rip-off? Would I make money off the stories? Would I make them into an American TV program? The next problem was religion, especially with elders. The old tales predate the arrival of Christianity or else treat it with sublime indifference. To tell them would label a person a heathen, wouldn't it? On a good many occasions I had to resolve this issue to the advantage of Our Lord before I could tap the narrative outlet. But by far the greatest difficulty lies with the times, which are a-changing, man. The people of the North are losing their stories along with their identities. Ugly as it may sound, they're becoming just like us. They've inherited our obesity, our *acne vulgaris,* our alcoholism, and our toys of progress. Near Gjoa Haven, Northwest Territories, I stayed in an Eskimo tent which was unheated, but which was equipped with the latest in stereo and video gadgetry. In other parts of Arctic Canada, the snow-machine has jostled aside the sled dog, though not without a certain nostalgia for the latter, since (as one Baffin man told me) you can't eat a snowmachine nor will it scent its way home during a blizzard. Even the blood feud has died out except for the odd incident, usually alcohol-inspired and subject to instant repent-

ence. Am I mourning the death of this violent tradition? Damn
right. At least it gave the people a specific *raison d'être*.

Once upon a time the boundary between animals and humans
was little more than a greyish blur. All living things had souls,
which migrated from one enchantment to the next, from a home
in one body, say, the body of a grizzled old musk ox, to a home in
another, such as the little girl next door. Then came the first
missionaries, who declared that animals do not have souls. By
their behavior it would appear that they did not think people had
them, either. Greenland's apostle Hans Egede whipped the
angakoks until they made public avowals of Christianity. Nor
were Hans Egede's Canadian brethren much better. They railed
against the Caribou Eskimo's belief that the basic human spirit,
inu'sia, inhabited a bubble of air in the (vile place!) groin; individ-
uals who were shown the light but went on professing this belief
were beaten, too. Prop by prop, the old edifice faltered. At last
only the foundation, the Woman of the Sea, remained. Called
Sedna or Nuliajuk in Canada, and Nerrivik in Greenland, she was
still the provider of all sea creatures. *Angakoks* continued to comb
her tangled hair and coax her with song. Then she too gave up the
ghost in favor of the Christian God. He could promise universal
salvation and a very pleasant afterlife; she could only promise
occasional respite from hunger. Yet rumor has it that there still
exists deep in the Arctic a small group of Woman of the Sea
devotees. They meet in secret and still send an *angakok* down to
comb the Woman's hair so that she'll bless them with game. Alas,
in all my travels, I never was able to substantiate this rumor.

But perhaps the last word should come from an old East Greenland storyteller named Anarfiik. I complained to him about the
loss of faith in the old myths. "Yes," he said, "the old myths are no
more." The Woman of the Sea herself was no more. *Ayuqnaq.*
Such are the ways of the world. Maybe one morning we will wake
up and the Christian God will be gone too. All a person can do is
live from day to day, a little rotten meat here, a bit of rancid seal

fat there, taking each moment as it comes. No cause for alarm. We were all going to die. *Ayuqnaq.*

And then Anarfiik told me a story, as if to proclaim: Here, my friend, is the only real ballast against the fragility of life and the nearness of death.

NOTE: Eskimo is a polysynthetic language wherein endless phrases can be strung together to form a single word. For example:

Parngnaniarsimavingmetovineonerartaujungnagalatsalungimarikpungalonelleq

This centipede of a word means something like: "I'm not sure that I want to go to jail." But that isn't the literal translation. If rendered into English literally, the word would be a battlefield of seemingly unrelated phrases. Bootless to try unless one is some sort of scholar. So it is with the tales in this collection. I've strived for readability rather than word-for-word accuracy. I've pared down localisms. Sometimes I've spliced together two or more versions of the same story. I've cut, polished, even recast. Ultimately, I wanted these stories to have the same immediacy that they might have if the reader were listening to the storyteller himself on a cold Arctic night.

I. Origins & Ancestors

The Woman of the Sea

IN THE TIME of the earliest forefathers, there lived a handsome young woman known far and wide for her long, thick hair. When she bunched this hair in a top-knot, it was almost the size of the rest of her body. Entire weeks she would spend combing it. Also, she had nice fat hands which many men admired.

One day this woman was picking berries when a fulmar flying overhead happened to see her. Immediately he swooped down and said:

"Marry me, my dear..."

The woman laughed and said sea-birds weren't much to her taste.

Then the fulmar went away and changed himself into a man. He put on a garment of the richest sealskin, a colorful tunic, and sun-spectacles made from walrus tusks. Now he came back and appeared at the woman's door. Once again he put the question to her.

"Well, you're a fine piece of man," she said, and left with him despite her parents' objections.

Now the woman lived with the fulmar in a little rock hut at the end of the sea. As she was fond of blubber, each day the fulmar would bring her a fresh seal. As she was fond of singing, he would sing to her while they made love. And so they had a happy marriage. But one day the fulmar's spectacles fell off and the woman saw his eyes. She said:

"You're just an ugly fellow, like all the others..."

All this time her parents had been paddling around in search of her. At every cove and headland they called out: "Daughter, daughter, where have you gone?" They searched the shore all the way to the Inland Ice. At last they arrived at the little rock hut at the end of the sea and beseeched her to return with them. She agreed to go. Because, she said, "I can't stand my husband's hideous eyes anymore."

Now the fulmar was searching for the woman himself. First he couldn't find her. But then he put on his walrus-tusk spectacles and saw the little boat in the sea below. Whereupon he flapped his wings wildly, more and more, and a terrible storm rushed over the water. Wind swept down the mountains. The boat looked as if it might capsize. The woman's parents said: "*You* brought on this storm. If you don't get out, we'll drown. Out, out with you!"

She protested that the storm was her husband's fault. It did no good. Her parents tossed her overboard. But she caught hold of the gunwale and clung to it. Her father took out his knife and cut off a few of her fingers. Still she clung there. He cut off a few more. Still she clung. And then he chopped off both her hands. She tried to hold on with her stumps, but she had no grip and as a result she slipped away. Immediately the waters subsided and her parents were able to paddle home, happy that they've survived even if it meant the sacrifice of their daughter.

The woman sank to the bottom of the sea. There she acquired her name Nerrivik, Food Dish. Her chopped-off fingers came back to her as fish, whales, seals, and walruses, all making their homes in her hair. But she couldn't comb this hair as she'd been able to before. Try as she might, she couldn't. For she didn't have any hands. All she could do was sit there at the sea-bottom, legs drawn up to her chest, and watch her hair get more and more filthy with each passing day.

Thus it is that *angakoks* must swim down to the depths and comb Nerrivik's hair for her. And, in her gratitude, she offers mankind all the creatures of the sea. The bounty in her long, spreading hair is endless. Friend, respect this woman.

Sun and Moon

THE MOON SLEPT with many women, but did not get pleasure from any of them. Then he decided to sleep with his pretty little sister, the Sun. He covered his face with ashes and slipped into her sleeping skins. Afterwards she said:

"Whoever you are, do it again..."

And so they did it again, all night long.

In the morning, the Sun learned the identity of her lover. Now she became quite upset. "You will never do this awful thing to me again, Brother," she said.

"Oh no? I am the stronger."

She picked up an *ulu* and cut off her breasts. Then she mixed her own urine and blood in a dish with the breasts and made *akutaq*. This she gave to her brother, saying: "Here, eat this if you want to see how I taste!" Then she dashed out of the house. The Moon paused to eat the breasts, and then went after her.

And still he pursues his sister, even today, to get her for his mate. But she is faster and always keeps well ahead of him. Thus, owing to the Moon's lust, does night follow day.

The Origin of Daylight

BEFORE THE TIME of the forefathers, the whole earth and all the heavens were covered in dark. Both the fox and the bear were men, and they met one day on an ice-floe. The fox said:

"Let there be light, for then I can see where the best seal breathing-holes are."

The bear replied:

"Let it stay dark, for I can sniff out the best seal breathing-holes in the dark."

The fox was the better *angakok*, the more cunning, the more powerful with words of the two. And thus daylight came into the world. The bear retreated to a dark ice-cave while the fox remained on the floes.

Since then human beings have been very grateful to the fox for making daylight and they do not eat fox meat unless they're starving.

The Louse and the Worm

IN THE BEGINNING, men did not have any lice on their bodies. The lice traveled about in tiny kayaks from fjord to fjord. Then one day a louse and a worm were paddling their kayaks and they decided to race toward land, to see who would be the first to climb onto man. Man's armpits were so warm and enjoyable that they chose them as their destination. Thus they could be heard as they paddled, shouting: "The armpits! The armpits!"

The worm was the better paddler, but his thongs broke owing to his powerful strokes. So the louse overtook him and came to land, and settled forever more in man's armpits. When the worm finally arrived, he crawled into the earth and hid there out of shame.

The Birth of Fog

ONCE UPON A TIME Glutton Spirits used to steal dead bodies and take them home to eat. It seems that nobody was safe in his grave those days. At last an *angakok* named Puagssuaq allowed himself to be buried alive, for he did not know who or what was making off with his people. But it was important to find out. Puagssuaq said:

"If the dead are not safe, neither are the living..."

Soon one of the Glutton Spirits saw the fresh grave, dug him up, and carried him back home. The Spirit had a wife and three children, all of whom were enormously fat. The wife went out to collect some firewood for the feast. The children gathered around Puagssuaq and one of them pinched him, saying:

"This human being is not dead, father. You can see how he moves when I pinch him."

"That's rubbish," said the Spirit. "He is just as dead as all the others. I would never bring home a live human being. That would be disgusting."

But he pinched Puagssauq himself, just to make sure. And he received a nasty surprise. The *angakok* sprang to his feet, saying:

"Earth, open up!"

And a hole opened up where the Glutton Spirit and his children were standing and all of them were sucked down into it, never to be seen again. The Earth closed over them. Whereupon Puagssuaq went out in search of the Spirit's wife. Soon he saw her, arms laden with firewood. Her cheeks bulged over her eyes so that she could hardly see and now she mistook him for her husband.

"I'll soon have supper ready for you, my dear one," she said.

Puagssuaq tried to stab her with his flensing knife, but she was so fat that it was like pricking a walrus with a bone-needle. At last she realized that he was not her husband. She said she would like nothing better than to tear his heart out through his mouth. Then she began to run after him as best she could. They ran until they came to a little river, which Puagssuaq jumped across. He stopped on the other side and said:

"Overflow your banks, little river!"

Now the woman could not get across. "How were you able to get across while I, a Glutton Spirit, am unable to do so?" she yelled.

He replied: "That's easy. I just drank up the water."

And now the woman began drinking the water. She drank until there was a dry path over which she could walk.

"*Ai!*" exclaimed Puagssauq. "What's that ugly thing sticking out of your vagina?"

The Spirit bent over to look and her stomach burst open from all that water. She dropped over dead. Steam came out of her, which turned to fog, the very first fog in the world. And because of this fog, human beings are safe in their graves today.

The Thunder Children

ONCE THERE WERE two children, a little boy and a girl, and they spent all their time playing directly outside the house. This used to annoy their stepfather, who claimed that he could never get any sleep. At last he said to them:

"Why don't you go and play somewhere else, you two? All that noise is driving me crazy..."

The two children, being fearful of their stepfather, wandered away far from home. They came to a remote mountainous place and then they began to play again:

"Let us turn into narwhals," the little boy said.

"No, no," his sister replied.

"Well, let us turn into walruses," he said.

"No, no..."

He mentioned all the animals of the sea and she didn't seem to care for any of them. Then he started in with the land animals:

"Let us become ice-bears!"

"I don't like ice-bears."

"Let us become reindeer, then."

"No, no..."

The boy ran out of animals. "Well," he said, "let us be transformed into thunder."

"Yes!"

And he kept shouting "let us be transformed into thunder" over and over again until they rose into the sky. And indeed they did turn into thunder. They pissed down on the land and it started to rain. The boy struck his firestone and there was lightning. And they made so much noise that thunder sounded everywhere in the world.

Finally their mother began to miss them. She said: "Are you not hungry, my children?" And she offered them her breast to suckle.

The children were indeed hungry. They came into the house, but the noise was so great that no one could tolerate it. The step-father dashed out, his hands over his ears. Their mother yelled at them please, please to go away. And so the thunder children returned to the sky and there they remained.

The Girl Who Married Her Dog

THERE WAS AN old couple who kept after their daughter to get married, but she kept telling them that she had not yet found the right man. At last her father was so annoyed at her that he said: "You'll never find the right man, daughter. Why don't you just take a dog for your husband?"

The girl did not reply, so her father repeated the question. At that moment the girl's dog rushed into the house. It proceeded to tear off her clothes and couple with her. The father took the dog outside and tied it up, but it broke loose from its traces and came in again and coupled with the girl again. Then the father rowed the dog to the other side of the fjord and left it there. This did not work, either. The dog simply swam across the water and again coupled with the girl. Now its penis got stuck inside her.

"I can see that the two of you are made for each other," the father said. And he rowed his daughter and the dog to a little island in the middle of the fjord. The island was nothing but rocks. There girl and dog lived, and at length the girl gave birth to a great litter of children, half human and half dog.

To get food, the dog would swim across the water with a pair of *kamiks* around his neck. The girl's father would put meat in the *kamiks* and then the dog would swim back to the island. One day the old man decided to put stones in the *kamiks*. He did this, and covered the top with meat. The dog started to swim back, but so heavy were the stones that he drowned before he reached the island.

The girl swore revenge for the death of her husband.

Now the old man got into the habit of rowing across the fjord with food for his grandchildren, of whom he was very fond. One day he rowed across and flung them their meat, but they still seemed to be hungry. The mother told them to lick the blood off the cover of the old man's kayak. Which they did. And then she smiled: "Eat him, my children!" And they knocked over the old man and quickly devoured him.

"Well done!" exclaimed the mother. But soon she was sorry, for her children had no source of food now. So she took the soles of her *kamiks,* made masts of whale-bone, and turned them into boats. Then she put her offspring in these boats. To one group, she said: "Go inland, and live on reindeer." These became Red Men. To another group, she said, "Go east, and plant your food in the dirt of the ground." These became White Men. She sent the rest of her children north. She told them: "You will not find much food to eat, so take whatever you can." And these became the Iniut.

Thus everyone is descended from these children. As for the girl herself, she stayed behind on the island. Having no meat, she starved to death. Her last days she spent thinking of her sweet little dog-children.

Sila, The Weather Spirit

IN THE OLD DAYS, a man came upon a giant baby dressed in reindeer skins and lying on the ground. Its head was the size of a boulder and its penis so big that four people could sit side by side on it. There was enough meat on this baby to feed the entire village for a winter.

Right away the giant baby seemed to know what the man was thinking. It said: "If you eat me, the world will come to an end."

The man laughed. And the baby went on:

"I am Sila, spirit of the wind and weather, lord of all places. When I shake these skins, the world itself shakes."

"Hah!" the man laughed, and took out his knife.

"If you don't believe me, just touch my little toe ..."

The man touched the baby's little toe. Suddenly snow began to fall from the sky.

"Now touch my head ..."

The man touched the baby's head. The snow fell more furiously, wind came, and the man was knocked off his feet.

"You see? No matter how hungry you are, you must never try to eat the weather ..."

And then the winds subsided and the baby slowly floated up to the roof of the sky. There it lived and there it shook its skin in earnest.

The Origin of Women

IN THE TIME OF floods and earthquakes, there was only one woman in all the world and she lived off by herself on a rocky island. She was an *angakok* who'd made her penis over into a vagina. Her name was Putu, Hole, and she was quite pretty as well. Once one of the mainlanders—a hunter named Qalaseq, Navel—traveled to her island in search of new hunting grounds. He did not get any game, but he did get Putu. And now he thought: I have a little wife, but the headman must sleep alone.

But then the headman came to the island, too. He stood outside the little hut and watched Qalaseq and Putu at their lovemaking. He thought: This looks rather nice... He watched until they had fallen asleep and then he grabbed Putu by the shoulders and began dragging her out of the hut. Qalaseq awoke just in time to catch her by the feet. And so the two men pulled at opposite ends of the woman until she broke in two. The headman carried away the upper part of her body, while Qalaseq kept the lower part with him on the island. Each carved the missing parts back to life out of walrus ivory and the thigh-bones of a bear. Now there were two living women, their bodies whole.

Right away the headman's woman made everyone in the village jealous. Why should this one man have a wife and everyone else sleep alone or with his dogs? So they began to pull at her until she likewise broke in half. And then they pulled at these two halves until there were four. And so on, until every man in the village had a woman of his own, each with her missing parts carved back to life. But soon they began to quarrel among themselves, as every man thought that the other's woman was superior to his own.

Qalaseq continued to live on the island with his woman, whom he now called Utssuajuk, Little-Big Vulva. She gave birth to six hundred fine, healthy children. But none of the women in the headman's village gave birth at all. Perhaps it was because they had been pulled apart too many times. Or perhaps there was some flaw in the ivory and bone out of which they were carved. No one knows.

The Origin of Wind

LONG AGO THERE was a huge ice-bear who carried a sack in which was kept all the wind in the world. He would not permit anyone to open this sack. But there was a hunter who was very curious about its contents. "What's in your sack?" he asked. "Just a big load of shit, that's all," the bear replied. "But why are you carrying it around?" the hunter said. "Who knows? I might get hungry while I'm traveling over the ice-floes..." The hunter did not believe this for a minute. He sang the bear to sleep and opened the sack. Out came the wind. It knocked the man down and sped away in all four directions. "Oh, Great Bear," the man said, "You can have my wife for a month, only get rid of this wind..." But it wouldn't have mattered if he had offered his wife for a full year. Wind had already entered the world.

The Pleiades

THERE WAS ONCE a woman whom no one would feed because she was menstruating. Her name is not given. She went into the mountains in search of food and at length she caught sight of a house made up of rock rubble. All around this house she smelled bear-scent. A voice called her from inside:

"Come in, little dear. We won't hurt you."

So the woman entered the house. Inside there was a family of bears in human shape. They had removed their skins, which were hanging in the house passage. The mother put on her skin when she went out to empty the urine-tub, but she took it off again as soon as she came back into the house. The children looked just like the children of human beings.

And now the mother asked the woman if she was hungry.

"I have not eaten in three days," the woman said.

They boiled some meat for her even though they ate it raw themselves. The father gave her blubber for her journey home-ward. And as she made ready to leave, he told her:

"Do not speak of us to your people. I have children and they deserve to grow up."

"I won't say a word," replied the woman.

She returned to her husband, And, of course, the first thing she did was to tell him about the bears. He became quite excited by the prospect of fresh meat. He made her lead him over the mountains to the place where the bears lived. After they got there, the woman hid behind a boulder.

Now the husband chanted:

> Meat, meat, meat, meat,
> Bring me meat, O Earth-Spirit...

The bears dashed out of the house with their children. But the children lagged far behind, so the mother killed them rather than let them fall into the hands of human beings. Then the woman's husband threw his harpoon and killed her as well. The he-bear approached him, saying this:

"Do not worry, little man. It is not you but your wife whom I despise."

And the bear dragged the woman out from her hiding place. He bit off her head and threw her body onto the midden-heap. Then he started to kick the head around as though he were playing ball with it. The husband's dogs chased after him and now he began to rise in the sky, still kicking the head. The dogs likewise rose, higher and higher, until they reached the very top of the sky. Whereupon bear and dogs became the constellation of the Pleiades.

Now the husband went back home. He had neither dogs or wife. He had only two little bear cubs and he had not even killed them himself.

The First Narwhal

IN THE STARVING TIMES, an old woman lived with her two grandchildren, a girl and a boy. The boy was blind from birth, but very strong. He could draw a bow as well as any hunter. Trouble was, he had nothing to draw it against. For game—even the smallest of birds, even worms, even maggots—seemed to have vanished altogether from the world.

One day, however, an ice-bear came sniffing around their hut. The grandmother told the boy: "I'll aim, you draw the bow. Perhaps we'll have a bit of luck."

And so she aimed and the boy shot the arrow. The bear dropped dead in its tracks.

Exclaimed the grandmother: "Too bad, boy. You missed. We'll just have to eat our *kamiks* for supper tonight..." Then she whispered to the girl not to let on to her brother about killing the bear. Two mouths were easier to feed than three. The blind boy would never know the difference.

But the girl saved some bear meat for her brother and gave it to him when the grandmother was asleep. As the boy ate, he developed a great thirst. He asked his sister to lead him down to the lake. Which she did. And to lay a path of stones back to their hut. Which she likewise did.

Now the boy drank and drank and could not stop drinking. All at once an enormous bird rose up from the depths of the lake. "Grab my neck," the bird said and after the boy had done this, it dove into the water. Four times it dove, each time with the boy hanging on to its neck. And each time they stayed longer and longer underwater.

"Notice anything?" the bird asked.

"*Aja,* I can...see!"

After the fourth dive, the boy could see everything with perfect clarity. He did not need the stones to find his way back to the hut.

"Well," said the grandmother, "since you can see now, perhaps you can do a little work around here..."

Now the three of them moved on and made a new camp by the sea. The boy spent his time on the shore searching for game. At last he saw a herd of whales swimming nearby. He called for his harpoon and tied the end of the line to his sister's waist. In this way, she became his partner and thus would be given a portion of any animal that he killed. But the grandmother objected. "Tie me up instead!" she instructed him.

And so he put the line around her instead of his sister. Then he threw his harpoon into one of the whales. The animal gave a jerk and pulled the old woman toward the sea. She grabbed at some roots, but they broke off in her hands. Soon the whale was dragging her along on the harpoon line. "Throw me my *ulu*! Throw me my *ulu*!" she yelled, hoping to cut the line. But by this time she was too far offshore, no matter how strong the boy's throw.

As she was pulled around in the water, the grandmother's hair was being twisted into a pigtail. And at the very moment she drowned, she turned into a narwhal—a male narwhal with a big twisted horn sticking out of its head.

The Father of Fish

TRAVELLER: Once in a while, if you wander far inland, you will chance upon an old man sitting by a river. This man has a big knife, but he does not intend it for you. Rather, he just sits there and whittles away at pieces of wood. All day and all night he whittles. All winter and all summer. The chips and splinters fly off and drop into the water, where they become alive. And by the time they reach the sea, they've turned into salmon, char, cod, capelin, lumpsuckers, and halibut. This man is the father of all fish. Do not kill him.

Mosquitoes

ONCE UPON A TIME mosquitoes couldn't have cared less about people. They kept to themselves on a remote little island and seldom paddled their kayaks more than a day's journey from this island.

But there was a man who robbed and cheated and stole his neighbor's wives. The last straw came when he stole an *umiaq* full of whale-belly. Thinking that no one would find him, he paddled away to the mosquito island. But his neighbors followed him and came to the island, too. They beat him to a pulp with their clubs and left him lying there on the rocks.

After that mosquitoes always attacked people, for now they had tasted human blood.

The Origin of Sharks

THERE WAS A GIRL named Qingaq who was madly in love. The man was a handsome young hunter and thus quite a catch. Every girl seemed to be wildly in love with him. And he took each of them in his turn. One day it happened to be Qingaq's turn. The man came up and said to her: "Tonight I will visit you in your hut." Now Qingaq wanted to make sure that she smelled especially nice for him, so she washed herself in a tub of urine. As she was drying her hair, a big gust of wind swept down and carried away the cloth. It carried this cloth over mountains and valleys, and over the Inland Ice. At last the cloth settled in the sea and there it changed into a Greenland shark. And so it is that shark flesh still has the odor of urine (it is not told whether Qingaq ever got the man she loved).

The First Walrus

IN THE TIME OF the forefathers, there lived a girl who always had a cold. She was forever coughing and sneezing. Snot streamed from her nose at all times. At last, since no man would have her, she married a raven. Her brothers did not like this, although one of them was married to an eagle and the other to a snowy owl. They went up to the raven's nest and took the girl back again. The raven was furious. He jumped up and down, flapping his wings and cursing mankind. Then he flew after them and reached them just as they were arriving home. He grabbed at the girl, but only got her legs, which came off. These he threw away. He grabbed again and this time he managed to get the rest of her. Now it was the brothers' turn to give chase. They pursued the raven back to his nest. However, he had made a new nest which was much higher than the last. The brothers could not reach it. All they could do was stand below and yell insults at him. "Hey, Raven! You smell of shit. Shit! It comes from your mouth..." "If you don't be quiet," the raven told them, "I'm going to drop a big boulder on you." "Your parents were shit, Raven. Shit comes from your mouth..." Meanwhile the girl decided that she didn't like the raven anymore because of what he had done to her legs. So she did her best to crawl out of the nest. It was not easy. All of a sudden she slipped and fell down, down into the sea. And when she came up again, the snot from her nose had hardened into a pair of tusks and she was a walrus.

Flies

ONCE THERE WAS a village where everyone had starved to death but a father and his son. These two were able to survive only by eating each other's lice. Soon, however, they ran out of lice. Now father and son paddled to another village and told about how they had kept themselves alive. No one believed them, since who can live off an exclusive diet of lice? Rather, it was said that they had eaten up all their neighbors. The villagers killed them and cut them open and found not a single piece of human meat in their stomachs—only lice. Then suddenly the lice came alive. They grew wings and flew out of the dead men and landed on the bodies of the living. In this manner, flies came into the world.

Of Giants and Human Beings

THERE WAS A giant so large that he could catch walruses in his bare hands. His wife was able to catch seals in her bare hands. This giant fell in love with an ordinary woman and asked her husband to trade wives with him. They did so. However, the man who slept with the giant's wife was pulled down into her and lost to sight forever. And the giant thrust his penis right through the woman and she died. Both giants were so ashamed that they gathered up their possessions and headed North. Nobody ever saw them again.

Killing People is Wrong

LIKE SO MANY of the forefathers, Poq liked to kill people. Once, after he had killed a harmless old man, his younger brother told him that he had to put a halt to his killing. Times have changed, the brother said, and now our numbers are getting too small for that sort of thing. Poq replied:

"I can't stop killing people. But from now on, I will kill only very little people."

And he began to remove the lice, one by one, from his body. Then he proceeded to kill them. After that he did the same thing to his brother's lice. In time, Poq killed more lice than anyone else among the forefathers.

II. Children

Kakuarshuk

LONG AGO women got their children by digging around in the earth. They would pry the children loose from the very ground itself. They would not have to travel far to find little girls, but boys were more difficult to locate—often they would have to dig extremely deep in the earth to get at the boys. Thus it was that strong women had many children and lazy women very few children or no children at all. Of course, there were barren women as well. And Kakuarshuk was one of these barren women. She would spend nearly all of her time digging up the ground. Half the earth she seemed to overturn, but still she could find no children. At last she went to an *angakok*, who told her, "Go to such-and-such a place, dig there, and you will find a child..." Well, Kakuarshuk went to this place, which was quite a distance from her home, and there she dug. Deeper and deeper she dug, until she came out on the other side of the earth. On this other side, everything seemed to be in reverse. There was neither snow or ice and babies were much bigger than adults. Kakuarshuk was adopted by two of these babies, a girl-baby and a boy-baby. They took her around in an *amaut* sack and the girl-baby lent her her breast to suck. They seemed to be very fond of Kakuarshuk. Never was she without food or attention. One day her baby-mother said: "Is there anything you want, Dear Little One?" "Yes," Kakuarshuk replied, "I would like to have a baby of my own." "In that case," her baby-mother replied, "You must go to such-and-such a place high in the mountains and there you must start digging." And so Kakuarshuk traveled to this place in the mountains. She dug. Deeper and deeper the hole went, until it joined many other holes. None of these holes appeared to have an exit anywhere. Nor did Kakuarshuk find any babies along the way. But still she walked on. At night she was visited by Claw-Trolls who tore at her flesh. Then there was a Scourge-Troll who slapped a live seal across her chest and groin. At last she could walk no further and now she lay down to die. Suddenly a little fox came up to her and said: "I will save you, mother. Just follow me." And the fox took her by the hand and led her through this network of holes to the daylight on the other side. Kakuarshuk could not remember a thing. *Aja*, not a thing. But when she woke up, she was resting in her own house and there was a little boy-child in her arms.

The Northern Lights Children

ONCE THERE WAS A hunter who kept losing his meat. He'd store a cache in his cave and next day it would be gone. The hunter was not too happy about this. He vowed to stab whoever was making off with his meat and then fling the lifeless body into the sea. And thus he hid himself in the back of the cave. One day passed, two days. Finally he saw a group of children who seemed to appear out of nowhere. They were gathered around his meat. Now the hunter was furious and he raised high his spear, hoping to kill each and every one of them. Then he realized: They were the Northern Lights Children—spirits of stillborn infants who danced with their afterbirths in the sky. They told him that they had been going through a very hungry season. Which was why he hadn't seen any Northern Lights lately. Wouldn't he allow them to take this meat? If not, the sky would be empty forever more. The hunter relented. "Please take what you want," he said to them.

And several days later there were Northern Lights in the sky once more.

The Child Who Lived in All Things

ONCE THERE LIVED a woman who gave birth to a stillborn child. As she did not wish to call attention to this, she crept out in the night and threw this child to the dogs, one of which promptly ate him. He was born again, yet as a dog. He lingered around middens and refuse heaps, and covered himself with snow in order to sleep. But he did not have the temperament of a dog and thus he obtained very little food. The woman was able to recognize her offspring. "You must learn to be more bold and push your way to the front," she said, "else you'll starve." And so the little dog was more bold. He scrapped with the others and fought for food. For his troubles, he was bitten on the snout. Whereupon he decided to enter the body of a bearded seal. Now he would not have to push his way to the front. He could catch fish whenever and wherever he wished. The seals were not afraid of death or man. Quite the contrary. They spent much of the day choosing which hunter would capture them (to be taken by a bad hunter was not dignified). But the child did not want to be captured just yet, so he escaped from his seal body and became a musk ox. Once again it was not difficult for him to obtain food. And musk oxen were very sociable animals. Unfortunately, they lived in constant fear of man. This fear the child could not tolerate, so he was born again as a walrus. Quickly he lost his fear of man. Now he had little to do but sit around lazily and grow fat. This bored him, so he changed himself into a raven. As a raven will eat anything, there was again plenty of food. And he felt a certain freedom soaring through the air or sitting on distant mountain crags. But he began to yearn for the sea. And since seals seemed to him to have the very best lives, he went into the body of a ringed seal. He married another ringed seal and sired many young seals. And at the end of his days, he allowed himself to be taken by a hunter whose wife was barren. The child slipped into her body just as he had slipped into the other creatures. Now the woman was pregnant. At last she gave birth to a strong, well-proportioned, handsome little boy. It was not surprising that this boy grew up to be a great hunter—he had already lived in the bodies of each and every creature that he hunted.

The Unwanted Child

IN THE HUNGRY TIMES, there lived a woman with seven children. She thought: I cannot feed another mouth. And so when the eighth child was born, she threw its body into the fjord. Then she began to observe all the taboos proper to a woman who'd had a miscarriage: she did not cut fat except with her feet; she did not speak unless spoken to; and so on.

Yet the unwanted child did not die. Quickly it picked up the skull of a dog, which it used as a kayak, and the thigh-bone of an old man, which it used for a paddle. Soon it went after its mother's brothers and tipped over their kayak. Both brothers drowned. Then the child returned to its mother and suckled her breasts. It slept happily in the midden outside the house.

A while later the child had tipped over a kayak belonging to the headman's son and the kayak of a man named Sangak, a gentle grandfather of a person. And each time it would return to its mother's breast and then spend the night in the midden.

It seems that everyone in the village who did not die of hunger now began to die by drowning. A *tupilak* was blamed, but the woman knew it was her child, flesh of her flesh, which was causing the trouble. At last she could not bear it any longer. She told her husband:

"I killed our child, and now it is coming back and killing everybody else."

And at that moment the child let out a loud scream and fell down dead in its midden heap.

The Boy Who Was Raised by Foxes

IN HUNGRY TIMES, a woman gave birth to a boy-child. She lent him her breast to suck. After a while, he grew tired of it. "That's nice, mother," the boy said, "but I would prefer some meat." So the father went out with his spear in search of game. He was caught in a blizzard and wandered from headland to headland. Indeed, he wandered around until he was quite lost.

The boy kept refusing his mother's breast. She offered him lice that she had picked off her own head, but he spat them out. Likewise he spat out the guillemot gruel she gave him. Poor dear, she thought, I'm afraid that you'll starve to death. So she went out to see what had become of her husband. She, too, got caught in a blizzard.

Now husband and wife searched for each other over a number of years. Up and down the coast they traveled. "Have you seen such-and-such a man? Have you seen such-and-such a woman?" they asked wherever they went. But no one seemed able to help them. Finally the woman visited an *angakok*, who located her husband on an island not far from Pangnirtung: he was visiting an *angakok* himself and man and wife could now see each other quite clearly. No blizzard this time. No wanderings in the rocky barrens. And at last they got together again and headed home to their son.

While the parents had been gone, some foxes had come to their hut. They found the little boy-child. But instead of eating him, they raised him as one of their own. They taught him everything a young fox needs to know in order to stay alive. He still looked like a human being, but on the inside he was a fox—perhaps more fox than most foxes are themselves.

Now the parents came back. They were quite delighted to find that their son was still alive. "Oh, dear son," they said, "you don't know how much we've missed you."

The boy was unable to speak or understand their language. Nor did he recognize them as his parents. He sniffed and growled and backed away. When his mother started to hug him, he bit her. For he had never before seen anything like his parents and he thought that they were two strange creatures who wished to kill him.

With sad hearts mother and father went away from that place. They never saw their son again.

Ussarqak, Who Ate Too Many Heads

LONG AGO THERE was a boy named Ussarqak who lived with his old grandmother. One day they ate the last of their food, and Ussarqak was sent out in search of something to eat. The first thing he found was a codfish. He pulled off its head and ate it. Then he walked some more, until he happened upon a bearded seal. Once again he pulled off the head and ate it. Then he saw a walrus. As before he ate only the head. He continued to walk and at length he came upon a stranded narwhal. "Ah, just what I was looking for!" Ussarqak said. And in the same manner, he pulled off the whale's head and ate it, blubber, bones, and all. Now he grew somewhat thirsty. He went over to a nearby lake and drank until the lake was dry. After which he belched contentedly and headed home. But now Ussarqak was so fat that he could not get through the door. "Try the window," his grandmother said. He tried the window and he couldn't get through that, either. Finally—strange to tell!—the old woman held up her needle and the boy passed through the eye of the needle with ease. However, he landed on the seal-oil lamp. There was a loud clap of thunder. The whole house exploded into a thousand little pieces. Where Ussarqak had been, there was only a big pool of water. And in this pool were a codfish, a bearded seal, a walrus, and a narwhal. All of them were swimming around quite happily except that they had only heads.

Qituarssuk

THERE WAS A GROUP of children playing at man-and-wife.
None of them would let the little Qituarssuk have a wife even
though he seemed to want one very badly. At last he began to cry:
"I want a little wife! I want a little wife!" But still they ignored
him, for—truth to tell—he was an orphan and not well-liked. So
he left them and climbed a steep hill. And from the top of this hill
he rolled down a boulder on his playmates and crushed not a few
of them. Whereupon the angry parents set out after the boy with
their spears. Qituarssuk hid behind another boulder and inside
this boulder he heard a strange voice speak: "Come in here, little
friend..." The people arrived with their spears, but they could not
find the boy. For Qituarssuk, having no other place of refuge, had
hidden inside the boulder. And he remains inside that boulder
even today. You can hear him still—still crying out for a wife.

Arviaq And the Worm

THERE WAS ONCE A woman named Arviaq who could not get with child. Her husband was a short little man with no strength in his loins. He told Arviaq: "If you want to be a mother, go find yourself a worm. They're much nicer than children, anyway." And so Arviaq found a worm and placed it against her breast as though it were a little child. She nursed it until she ran out of milk and then she nursed it under her armpits. Soon the worm began to grow large. And the larger it grew, the thinner Arviaq became. All her blood was going into her offspring. And all her love, too— often she would spend the whole day at home, fondling and kissing the worm. At last it was large enough to crawl around the village. This did not make people very happy, because it had sharp teeth and a rather unpleasant disposition. One day the headman and a few others took their knives to it. Spurts of blood as high as a house shot up from its body and the worm shriveled back to its original size. Poor Arviaq watched all of this and afterwards beat her head against a rock, crying, "My dear little child, my dear dear little child."

Qalaganguase,
Who Had No Strength

ONCE THERE WAS A boy named Qalaganguase who lived at a
place where the tides were quite powerful. His father drowned,
and then his mother. His sister looked after him for a while, but it
wasn't long before she drowned, too. Then there were only
strangers to look after him.

As he grew up, Qalaganguase had strength neither in his loins
nor the rest of his body. He always stayed home while the others
were away hunting. Women mocked him. Little children made
small of him. Then one day he was sitting at home, and he heard a
frightful sound. He went to hide behind the skin hangings. Soon a
ghost entered the room, walked over to the water tub, and lifted it
to his mouth, drinking heartily.

"Such did I drink when I lived here once," the ghost said. And
then it vanished out the door.

Time passed. Once again the people were all away hunting and
Qalaganguase was sitting alone in the house. Now the walls
started to shake and a large crowd of ghosts danced in, one after
another, and the last one was Qalaganguase's sister. The ghosts
sat on the floor and wrestled and told stories, all that sort of thing.

"Such did we play when we lived here once," they said.

At first Qalaganguase feared them, then he saw that this was
not a bad way to pass the night.

"If you tell your people about us," the ghosts said, "strength will
never come to your loins. However, if you keep quiet, you'll
become a very healthy young man." And then they walked away
into the snowy night. The last to leave was Qalaganguase's sister,
who kissed him goodbye. The hunters were just returning home

and they saw a pair of dainty little feet vanishing in the passage-way.

"Whose feet were those?" they said.

"Oh, they only belong to the ghost of my sister," replied Qualaganguase. 'You see, ghosts have been coming to this house and they say that I am to grow strong..." At that, he felt even weaker yet. For he had betrayed the ghosts who were now taking away what little strength he had.

"Hah!" the people laughed. "You will always be little Qalagan-guase, who is lame in the body and lame in the loins." And they went off to a drum-song contest and left him all alone again. Poor Qalaganguase lay down on the bed and began to sob. Soon the ghosts of his dead parents came to visit him.

"What are you doing here all alone?" they asked him.

"It is because I am so weak," he told them.

"Perhaps you should come away with us," his parents told him.

"Yes, perhaps that's best..."

And they took him to the Land of Ghosts where he became a ghost himself. It is said that when he was changed into a ghost, Qalaganguase became a woman. He was never seen on earth again.

The Spoon Monster

ONCE THERE WERE SOME children who were playing at the shore. They were just minding their own business when all of a sudden Qalutligssuaq the Spoon Monster rose up from the sea. He made his usual noises, which sound like spoons being smashed together. The children screamed and shouted and dashed away . . . all except one little boy, who was lame and could not run as fast as the others. Qalutligssuaq soon overtook him. The boy fell to the ground and began waving his toe back and forth in front of the monster, saying:

"Watch out for my big toe, friend! Watch out for my big toe! It might very well eat you . . ."

The monster was terrified and headed back to the sea. And ever since then Qalutligssuaq has been repelled by this same way: For what could be more terrifying than a big toe waggling back and forth, back and forth?

Tulugaq, Who Was Barren

IN THE TIME OF the forefathers, there lived a childless woman named Tulugaq who was always being mocked by her two sisters. "Barren! Barren!" they would laugh at her. Indeed, everyone laughed at Tulugaq because she was barren. At last she visited the *angakok*. She told him that she wanted a child more than anything else. She said that she wanted a child so badly that she didn't care what it looked like. Whereupon the man went into a trance and contacted his *toornaq*, a walrus. This *toornaq* flew down to the place where all children yet-to-be were hidden. He returned with a frown on his face. Then the *angakok* told the woman:

"You will be given a child, but you must never, never look at it..."

A while later, Tulugaq did bear a child. She bound it up in sealskin so she wouldn't have to look at it. However, she was so secretive about it that her husband thought there might be something wrong. He pulled open the sealskin and let out a loud scream and fell over dead.

Then her two sisters came for a visit. They were curious about any child that Tulugaq could bring into the world. Tulugaq warned them, but they looked anyway. Both screamed and they fell down dead, their heads sliced off their bodies. "I told you not to look," Tulugaq said.

At this point, the *angakok* wanted to know what sort of child was causing all the trouble. His *toornaq* had not described it to him in any detail. So he went to Tulugaq. "You told me that I should never look at it," she said, "so I don't think you should, either." But he didn't listen to her. He pulled back the sealskin and he likewise died. His eyes were dripping from their sockets.

Now Tulugaq and her child were thrown out of the village. She took to wandering the mountains, the child in an *amaut* on her back. All this time she was growing more and more curious about the child. Finally she had to look at it. She pulled back the sealskin. And she saw a creature made of stone, with flensing knives for fingers and sharp ribs sticking like walrus tusks from its chest.

"I beg you not to harm me," she said to it, "because I am your dear little mother..."

This did not seem to make any difference. Tulugaq fell over dead like all the rest. Then the creature climbed out of its skins. It searched around for something to eat, but it did not know how to get food for itself. Soon it became very hungry, and cried out:

"Mother, mother..."

But there was no mother anymore. After it starved to death, Tulugaq's child turned from stone to sand and strong winds came along and blew this sand off the face of the earth.

The Monstrous Child

IT WAS IN THE starving times, and a man and woman had a child. The mother fondled it. The father said many kind things to it. But as they never fed it meat, the child did not grow. What little meat they had, they kept for themselves. Nor did they smear even a bit of suet around its little mouth. *Aja*, not even suet—when the child cried out, the parents simply fondled it.

And so it happened that one night this child began to eat its father and mother while they lay there sleeping. It ate them both up, head to foot. Then it crawled out of the house, crying:

"I've eaten my parents because they wouldn't feed me. Now I'd like to eat my sister and elder brother, too..."

"But haven't I given you water and some berries?" the sister said.

The child devoured her as well. Now its mouth was dripping with blood and fat. And when people saw this, they leaped up and fled, all but the child's elder brother, who went for his knife. Just as he stabbed it, the child repeated: "*Aja*, they would not feed me..." And then it died, belly bloated up with its parents and sister.

Anarteq

AN OLD MAN had a good many daughters, and one son named Anarteq. The man loved the daughters, but he loved his son yet more. If anything happened to the boy, he knew that he would have to go hunting again as though he were a boy himself. He preferred to remain at home, singing old songs to the wallskins.

Many were the times when Anarteq would climb into his kayak and his sisters into their *umiaq* and all would paddle to the reindeer hunting ground. Once there, the girls would yell and wave sticks and drive the reindeer to the edge of the fjord. Anarteq would be sitting in his kayak and he'd launch one harpoon after another at them. In this fashion, they would have their boats well laden with meat by the end of the day.

One day Anarteq launched one of his harpoons at a reindeer that had broken away from the rest. The spear struck the animal in the flank. The reindeer burst into the water and, swimming away, knocked over Anarteq's kayak. The boy struggled, but he could not roll the kayak over again. Thus he had to ease his way out of it. But he could not swim a stroke. His sisters looked on helplessly from the shore.

"It's all over with me, dear sisters, for the salmon already have begun to eat my stomach."

"We'll go and get father," the sisters said.

"Too late," replied Anarteq, "for now they're eating my intestines."

And then he fell asleep. When he woke up, he was a salmon heading with other salmon toward the open seas. Anarteq thought: If I have to be another creature, I might as well be a salmon.

The old man mourned his son for twice the usual mourning period. Then he made ready to go hunting. Else his daughters would not have meat or blubber to eat. Or even marrow to suck.

Some years passed, and the father—however feeble—was still hunting. His daughters were doing the rowing for him. One day he was hunting reindeer in the same fjord where Anarteq was drowned. He began to weep upon thinking of his son. Suddenly he felt something hit the bottom of the boat. He jabbed at it with a paddle. He felt one tug, then two, very strong. Then he saw that there was a large salmon with its mouth around the end of the paddle. "It's Anarteq! It's our brother!" the girls exclaimed.

And the old man drew up the paddle with the salmon still attached to it. As the salmon landed in the boat, it turned into Anarteq himself. He had gone into the sea as a boy and now he was a man—a big robust man dressed in a coat of the finest sealskin. He said:

"Sit down, father. It's my turn to do the hunting now..."

And the old man handed the son his harpoon.

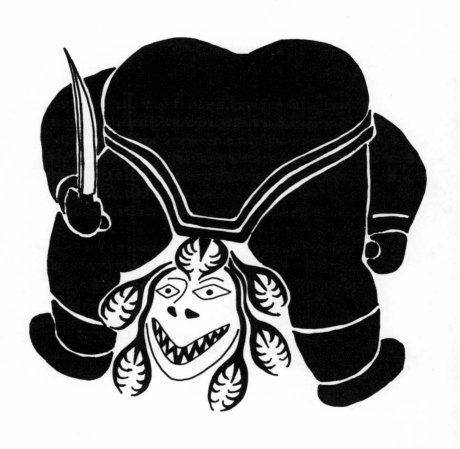

III. Magic & Taboos

"The Earth Will Know"

A WOMAN GAVE BIRTH to a creature of the twilight, all splotched and bristly-skinned, which no one could seem to identify. The *angakok* said: "The Earth will know." So they killed the creature and buried it in the ground, to learn what kind of thing it was. The ghost came back: a pretty little girl.

Every Taboo is Holy

A WOMAN NAMED Oruneq was giving birth to a child. It was not an easy birth, so an *angakok* helped her, chanting: "Fly out, little creature. Fly out like a sledge over smooth ice..." As the child began to ease out, the mother said: "May you always have meat, my little one." Then she licked it and wrapped it in rabbit skins with outward-facing fur. Into this fur she sewed the end of her navel cord. All the while her other children were standing outside the hut and dancing first on one leg, then the other.

Oruneq obeyed all the taboos. She covered her head with her *amaut* and did not burn a blubber lamp for eight days. Every bite of food she took for herself, she rubbed against the child's mouth first. Even so, the child grew thinner as well as longer with each passing day. It played a game with itself in which it made coils out of its own body. Finally the child turned into a worm and slithered away, never to be seen again.

The woman cried, but she knew what had happened: Once, during her pregnancy, she had eaten a meal of reindeer intestines. If you eat intestines during your pregnancy, your child will turn into a worm, too.

The Sick Raven

THE GREAT ANGAKOK Ulilik once came upon a sick raven. The bird had a terrible belly-ache and could scarcely move owing to the pain.

"It must have been something you ate," Ulilik said.

"That's true," said the raven. "We're not supposed to eat human meat and animal meat in the same week. But I happened to eat a baby's corpse and the very next day I followed it up with some reindeer meat..."

And now, the raven added, he was paying the price for not obeying a taboo.

The great *angakok* took pity on him and cured him at once. The raven thought for a moment about the sort of gift he should offer the man in return. At last he presented Ulilik with the best thing he could think of—a nice fresh gob of raven shit.

Meaning: What's shit to one creature is bounty to another.

The House of Reindeer

ONCE AN *angakok* was asked by his people to find the place
where reindeer went when they left the coast. Somewhere within
the Inland Ice was this place, but no one ever traveled there for
fear of the Dog-Headed People. The *angakok* went into a trance
and contacted his *toornaq*. The *toornaq* told him: "Yes, I know all
about the house of reindeer. It will be no problem for me to lead
you there."

And so the *angakok* set out on a journey to the Inland Ice. He
traveled for two full moons. It was a tough trip, but his boots and
trousers stayed fit because his *toornaq* was with him, always
mending them. Along the way, he saw quite a few of the Dog-
Headed People. They did not take bites out of his thighs or that
sort of thing. In fact, they left him alone for he could make
himself invisible whenever he wanted. Nor did he have any difficulty with Thrashing Spirits for the same reason.

One day his *toornaq* said: "We will stop here until dusk. Then
you will see the house of reindeer. But I warn you: You must
neither kill any of them or have the wish to kill any of them."

"And what happens if I do kill one of them?"

"I will transform you into the lowest creature on earth..."

At dusk the *angakok* found himself standing beside an enormous ice-house. There was a herd of reindeer grazing on a nearby
nunatak. Each reindeer, after it had finished grazing, would head
into the house. The man stayed there all night and the herd
seemed without end. It was the most beautiful thing he had ever
seen.

At length he went back over the ice to his own home. People
asked him about his trip, but he did not dare tell them about the

beautiful place he had visited. For they would journey there right away and kill all the reindeer. And then his *toornaq* would have no choice but to transform him into a maggot.

The Cure

IN FROBISHER BAY, a certain *angakok* got his gift in this fashion: he'd been struck on the head by lightning when he went out to ease his bowels. Now he was called Burnt-Head and he could tell which children would live and which die. Owing to his experience with the lightning, this Burnt-Head had come to believe that all things in the world have their origin in shit. One day a man visited him and said: "My little daughter is very sick. Each day she gets weaker and weaker. Soon she will die." "Bring me some of your daughter's shit," Burnt-Head said. The man did as he was told, and the *angakok* ate the little girl's shit. In fact, he ate the little girl's shit for an entire week. And the more he ate, the less weak was the little girl. At the end of the week, she was cured and could dance and play and such-like. Burnt-Head, however, had become quite ill. He could hardly move, much less embark on spirit flights. He complained to a friend who was also an *angakok* that he felt like he was about to die. "Never fear," the other said. "I can cure you." Burnt-Head was dubious, but less so when his friend asked for some of his shit.

Katerparsuk, The Orphan

ONCE THERE WAS A boy named Katerparsuk. Being an orphan, he was forever the victim of taunts. His chief nemesis was a man named Sammik. Sammik would walk up to Katerparsuk and cuff him across the mouth, saying, "Why don't you go take a jump into the sea, silly orphan boy?" Once Katerparsuk was trying to build himself a kayak. No one would lend him a knife, so he was using shells and stones for his tools. Sammik disguised himself in a bearskin and crept up on the boy and growled loudly in his ear. The boy fled in terror, and Sammik threw his shells and stones into the sea. Everyone thought that this was quite funny.

Now as the boy became older, he began studying to be an *angakok*. He spent much of his time by himself, practicing magic—first small magic, like flying through the air, and then larger magic. At last he was able to fly down to the underworld. He went down there and saw his dead parents and dead little sisters. They were collecting berries on a hillside. After giving him berries and *kiviaq* to eat, they implored him to remain with them, saying that life was better after death. "I'll come again when I die," he told them. "Right now I'm only here on a practice flight..."

Some years passed, and now Katerparsuk had learned to chant the skin off animals—first small animals, like insects, and then larger ones. One day he saw a big walrus diving in the water and he chanted louder and louder until the walrus cast off its skin. Katerparsuk put on this skin and he swam through the water just like a walrus. Hunters saw him, but he found that he could harden his skin so that no harpoon would penetrate it.

Meanwhile Sammik had grown into an old man. He was far too feeble to hunt. For the most part, all he could do was row out to a fishing-place and drop his line in the water. Once he went to this fishing-place and Katerparsuk swam up to him in his walrus suit. "He looks so easy to kill!" thought Sammik. And he paddled home and collected his harpoon. Then he paddled back to where he had seen this enormous walrus. The animal was still there. The old man threw his harpoon, but Katerparsuk hardened his skin and the harpoon-point bounced off. Katerparsuk then took the harpoon and bladder float with him to the bottom of the sea. Sammik had to paddle home empty-handed.

That night Katerparsuk gave a feast in his hut to which Sammik was invited. The old man went on and on about the walrus he'd been hunting. It was the largest, most violent creature in the sea. It had given him a terrible fight. At last it had dragged off all his hunting implements. Then Katerparsuk produced the harpoon and bladder float, and said:

"This silly old man is imagining the whole thing. There was no walrus at all. I had to take these things away from him because I was afraid that he'd hurt himself."

Everyone in the hut thought that this was quite funny. Everyone except Sammik, who was the orphan now.

Bad Food

ONCE A DEAD WHALE washed up on Disko Island. It was half-buried in the snow by the time anyone found it. As this was the starving times, people were delighted. For weeks they came down and cut off huge chunks of the whale which they brought back to their stewpots. They said it was the best meat they'd ever eaten. Slowly the snow cleared away from the whale. Finally there came a day when people saw underclothes and *kamiks* on its body. "No whale wears underclothes and *kamiks*," said the *angakok*, "we have been eating a giant..." And one by one people began to die. Indeed, everyone died except for one old man who had no teeth and thus was unable to chew meat: All the while he'd been living off scurvy-grass, ptarmigan droppings, and his own lice.

The Rival Angakoks

IN THE OLD DAYS, two *angakoks* named Sammik and Apilak were always fighting. Each thought himself the more powerful. Each thought that he could fly through the air better than the other. Sammik thought he could erase wounds from a sick person's body more quickly than Apilak. Apilak thought he could chant game into submission better than Sammik. At last Sammik decided to take action. He fashioned a *tupilak* from fur and bones and sent it against his rival. But Apilak, who was adept at such things, sent back the *tupilak*.

Now Sammik was hunting ringed seals in the fjord. He was not having much luck. Then he happened to see a large seal swimming near the surface. He threw his harpoon into it, killing it. But after he had flensed the seal, he noticed that the bones were all out of place. The skull was in the tail, the flippers in the ears, and the spine made up of ribs. He had harpooned his own *tupilak*...

Whoever harpoons a *tupilak* is doomed. Sammik fell directly to the ground. In a short while, his legs would not move. Then his arms went stiff. Now his mother had to feed him because he could not provide for himself. In the end, he could not even move his jaws to eat food. He died of hunger.

Apilak celebrated his rival's death with a flight to the moon.

The Spirit of the Shit-Pile

ONE NIGHT A little girl was playing with her sealskin dolls. She heard a husky voice at the window: "Come play with me, little girl. I have far prettier dolls than you." The husky voice belonged to the Spirit of the Shit-Pile. He lived in a little hut inside the shit-pile which was behind her parents' hut.

Now she went with him, and brought her dolls with her. He seemed like a very kind spirit. He said: "Just lay your head on my lap and I'll pick the lice from it." She did as he said, placed her head on his lap, and he pulled out a needle and thrust it through her ear. She died right away. Then he put her dead body beneath his sleeping platform.

Next day the boy who was the little girl's brother heard a voice calling him: "Come with me, little boy. I have a very fine harpoon head to give you..." And he too went with the Spirit into the little hut inside the shit-pile. The Spirit brought out his needle and was ready to stick it into the boy's ear when the boy said: "Don't kill me. Here, take my *kamiks*." The Spirit took his *kamiks*.

"Now take my mittens and coat."

The Spirit took his mittens and coat. Now the boy was completely naked. The Spirit drew out his needle again, but the boy said: "You must not kill me because I am the only hunter in the family. My old parents will starve to death if you kill me."

At that the Spirit took pity on the boy and told him that he could go. As he was leaving, the boy saw the body of his little sister under the sleeping platform. But he didn't say a word about it lest he endanger himself again. Instead he told his parents who told everyone else in the village. And nowadays no one ventures into a shit-pile.

The Entrail Thief

ONCE THREE MEN journeyed to the edge of the Inland Ice to hunt reindeer. As the reindeer were plentiful, they decided to stay there for a while. So they made a comfortable little ice-hut. They were fast asleep one night when an old hag came to visit them. She was Aukjuk, stealer of entrails. And she passed directly through the ice of their hut. Dish in hand, she walked up to the first man and sucked out his entrails as he lay in his sleeping skins. She did the same thing with the second man. And the same thing with the third man as well. She put all their entrails in her dish and headed back out through the ice again.

Now the men became so light that they proceeded to rise into the sky, right up to the moon. Once they landed, they went straight to the House of the Man in the Moon and complained about their ill-treatment. "Intestines and such-like are very important to us human beings," they said. "I know nothing about this," the Man told them. "You must see Aukjuk." And so they went outside and saw Aukjuk, who was preparing supper. "Oh, please don't eat our entrails," they told her. But she had already begun to cook the Man in the Moon's supper. Their entrails were the main course.

The men had to return home to their wives all hollow inside. Such is the punishment for those who visit the ice-edge.

Him-Whose-Penis-Stretches-Down-To-His-Knees

HIM-WHOSE-PENIS-STRETCHES-DOWN-TO-HIS-KNEES did not observe the proper taboo when he slept with his wife just after he handled a corpse. His wife mentioned this, but he only laughed and pointed to his penis, saying:

"That big fellow knows nothing about taboos."

The very next day he was walking by the fjord. A huge raven rose up from some boulders and grabbed at his penis and tore off a piece of it. Then the raven flew away with this piece dangling from its beak.

Him-Whose-Penis-Stretches-Down-To-His-Knees soon came to be known as Him-Whose-Penis-Barely-Peeps-From-Its-Cave. He had learned his lesson: Now he would not even sleep with his wife the same week as he handled a dead body.

"I am only shit!"

A WOMAN WAS menstruating and thus no one would give her anything to eat. One day she caught sight of a whale far out in the sea. She had become quite hungry, so she waved her hands and exclaimed: "I am only shit! I am only shit!" And the whale began to swim toward her. Soon it swam out of the water and onto dry land, right beside her. "I am only shit," she said. And the whale died.

Such holy words!

The Brother-in-Law
Who Became A Bear

FIVE MEN DECIDED to go hunting together. Four of them were brothers, and the fifth had taken their sister to wife. The men journeyed out of the fjord, onto the floe-ice, to a place well-known for its seals. They had been sitting for only a short while when the ice suddenly broke. Then the men were borne on a little ice island farther and farther from land. And then the ice island started to melt. The men turned to the eldest brother, an *angakok*, and asked him for help. He called upon his *toornaq*, an ice-bear, and in turn asked it for help. The *toornaq* said no problem. The floe tipped up, and the men slipped off and into the sea. And as each slipped off, he was transformed into an ice-bear himself. Now all of them were swimming through the water with great ease. Soon they came upon some seals. "You mustn't kill any of these seals," the *angakok* said, "till we become men again." But the brother-in-law was too hungry to pay heed to his words. He swam after a seal, killed it and ate it in about three bites. The others swam to the shore and were transformed into seagulls so that they could fly home. Once home, they turned back into men. Not the brother-in-law. He climbed onto the shore and he was still a bear. He was unable to turn back into a man now. Indeed, he remained a bear for the rest of his life.

Meaning: It's not a good idea to kill game when an enchantment destroys all the odds.

A Tale of Motherlove

BEING A GIANT, Sikiliaq was too heavy to go on the ice and hunt. So he would wait on land and when hunters came back, he would seize their seals. This happened so often that people started to grow hungry. They decided to put an end to Sikiliaq. One day they grabbed him and tied him up and dragged him onto the ice. As he was thrashing about, he broke the ice. And sank like a boulder to the bottom of the sea.

Now Sikiliaq's mother was not too happy about her son's death. He was her first born. She told the men who had killed him: "When you take a piss, don't look up or you'll die . . ."

They merely laughed at her. Silly old woman. Little did they know that she had *angakok* powers. And as each man emerged from the house, a crow cawed. Each man looked up and, pissing, died. The last man came out. The crow cawed, but he did not look up. The crow cawed again, and again no result. Since she couldn't kill the man, the woman decided to marry him.

The man had just finished his piss and he saw this beautiful young woman standing in front of him. She was the giant's mother, who had sung a spell on herself. The man liked the looks of her. In fact, he liked the looks of her so much that he took her to wife. She used her magic again and bore a son after only a month. She pulled the boy's knuckles and fed him reindeer sinew to make him strong. Within a few months, he was fully grown.

Not long after the boy's first birthday, he visited his father in a seal blind. "Come sit beside me, dear son," the man said, "and I'll show you how to catch a seal." The boy did as he was told. Then he brought out a drill which he had made from a narwhal tusk. He burrowed a hole into his father's skull and sucked out the brains and spat them into the sea. Same with the heart, lungs, and entrails, all of which sank to the bottom of the sea.

Thus, by the death of her husband, did Sikiliaq's mother get even for the killing of her son.

The Feasting House Ghost

THERE WAS ONCE A GIRL and she was sent by her parents to fetch some dried fish from their feasting house. Since it was very late at night, she could not see the dried fish or anything else. She muttered to herself:

"It's a good night for ghosts..."

Now as she was feeling around in the dark, she happened to touch a male body. The body was not wearing any clothing.

"I bet you're a feasting house ghost," the girl said.

"That's right," came the answer, "and now you're touching my nose...now you're touching my ears...now my mouth...my chest...my navel...now my penis...and now my testicles..."

Then the ghost grabbed the girl and started to strangle her.

"At least let me get a piece of dried fish before you strangle me," the girl remarked.

"All right," the ghost said. But as soon as he let go of her, she dashed out of the house and ran back home.

The girl learned her lesson, which was: One should never ask after a ghost. To do so obliges the ghost to appear.

Don't Forget to Pray

YOUNG PERQANAQ, having killed a narwhal, forgot to pray to its departed soul. Soon a crack in the ice split his house in half and he did not see his family for eight years. Nights, Claw-Trolls would come and scratch at his flesh. Sometimes he was thrashed by the Thrashing Troll and sometimes the *Amaut* Witch nibbled at his ears. A Glutton Spirit ate away the meat from his body. For three years, he lived on an island where the only food was lichens and snails. He had no female company.

All of which taught Perqanaq a lesson. Now he prays even to the souls of lice which he picks from his body.

Niarqoq

THERE WAS ONCE AN *angakok* named Niarqoq who could do all sorts of miraculous things. He went on spirit flights that allowed people to gaze up and see his heart dangling through his ass. He could turn himself into a tiny maggot so that his entire body would be able to enter a woman's vagina. He could even pull off his own genitals and replace them again. One day this Niarqoq went out hunting with some companions. It wasn't long before he saw a big ice-bear. He threw his harpoon just as the bear swatted at him. Niarqoq's intestines fell out. Then the bear swatted at him again. One of his arms came off. Then the bear took an enormous bite out of him. There was a gaping hole in his chest. By now his companions figured that he was dead. But not Niarqoq, son of Oqortoq! He simply entered the body of the bear and lived there happily ever after.

Namik

NAMIK LACKED ALL WISDOM. He went out to hunt during a plague of shooting stars. The stars dripped down on him just a little. But this was enough to transform poor Namik into a greyish patch of lichen forever.

Moral: Remain indoors or the star shit will get you.

The Lame Man's Stick

THERE WAS A MAN who had an accident with a cliff—he fell off it. Now he could walk only with the aid of a stick. This made it somewhat difficult for him to hunt. One day he and his wife had no food in the house except for seaweed and some mussels. He said: "Don't worry, woman. I will find some fat for you to chew."

Then he hobbled as best he could toward the ice-floes. Soon he saw the tracks of a bear and before long he came upon the bear itself, tearing apart a spotted seal. The lame man went right up to the bear and chanted these words in its ear:

> "Strong man of the sea,
> May sleep invade your eyes.
> Strong man of the sea,
> May you fall asleep forever.
> Strong man of the sea,
> May you be meat..."

Whereupon the bear fell asleep instantly. The lame man lifted its tail and thrust his stick deep into its ass. This woke up the bear. It roared and started toward him. But he pushed it back on the stick, which went through its body like a harpoon, killing it. After which he loaded the carcass onto his sledge.

Then did the stick begin to move of its own accord, over ice and toward the village, dragging the sledge along with it. The stick went up to the lame man's wife and tapped her on the shoulder, saying, like her husband, "Now you will have fat, woman."

And that was not all—soon the stick was going out to hunt all by itself. The lame man would stay at home and the stick would return with reindeer, seals, and fresh walrus. No one in the village could sniff out game better. For the stick had acquired the powers of a bear because it had entered the bear's holy of holies, the ass.

Erdlaversissoq

A MAN AND WOMAN died in short order when an avalanche came down and crushed their ice-hut. Whereupon they began the ascent of the tall mountain which leads to the other world.

"We must watch out for Erdlaversissoq, and not laugh at her," said the woman.

Replied the man: "Now that I am dead, I will do what I please..."

Finally they reached the mountain top. Here the famous spirit Erdlaversissoq lived, huge of ass and grotesque of manner. She stood before them beating her drum and dancing with her shadow. She sang: "Great is my ass, great is my ass..." Every once in a while she'd lean over and lick herself between the buttocks. Also from between these same buttocks dangled a whole family of sea-scorpions. She had a nose in the middle of her forehead.

The man could not help himself—he laughed. Then Erdlaversissoq stopped dancing and brought out her knife. The man found that he was unable to move. She cut him open and thrust his entrails all at once into her mouth, chewing heartily. When she had finished, she flung the husk of his body back down the mountain. He came to rest on a heap of rocks, where he remained, never buried, always homeless.

But the man's wife, who had not laughed, managed to continue on and enter the other world. And even now she lives there happily, eating *mataq* and berries and singing old songs with the other dead people.

The Glutton

ATUNGAIT LOVED to eat so much that his belly grew quite vast. He tried to tighten it with thongs so that it would not drag behind him—but it always popped out again. He even tried to stick it in a hole in the ground. At last he decided that he needed another belly. And as he was a notable *angakok*, he told a mountain: Henceforth, O mountain, you shall be my new belly. Now he had a much larger place to store his food. He did not need to share it with anyone. The biggest belly in the world was his. Yet a sad thing happened one day while Atungait was out walking under his mountain: An avalanche killed him.

Imarasugssuaq

ONCE UPON A TIME there lived a man named Imarasugssuaq who had a habit of eating his wives. First he'd fatten them up, then he'd kill them and toss them in the stewpot. He disposed of many wives in this manner, yet women kept on marrying Imarasugssuaq because he was a very handsome fellow.

Once, having just eaten a wife, he took to wife a woman named Kalakavsiq. Soon he was feeding her walrus fat, only walrus fat, day after day. This Kalakavsiq, who was a thin woman, began to grow fat. The more walrus, the fatter she got. Finally she was so fat that she could barely make it through the door. Well, she thought, I'll be my husband's supper if I don't think of something soon. She waited until he went hunting in his kayak. And then she took her breeches and tunic and stuffed them with wiping moss until she had made a dummy which resembled a woman. She said to this dummy:

"When my husband comes home, this is what you must say to him. 'I cannot move because I've become too fat.' Then he'll harpoon you. Remember to cry out in pain..."

After giving these instructions to the dummy, she dug a hole at the back of their hut and buried herself in it.

Imarasugssuaq came home later that night. "I'm hungry, woman," he said. "Go and bring me some *kiviaq*."

Replied the dummy: "I can't move. I'm too fat."

"Better a fat wife than a dish of rotten guillemots," he exclaimed. Then he thrust his harpoon into the dummy wife, who cried out as though in pain. He thrust it again. The dummy cried again. Well, another dead wife, thought Imarasugssuaq. And he picked up the dummy and tossed it into the stewpot. It was not even fully cooked when he ate it, clothes, wiping moss, and all. Soon he became quite sick. He lay on the ground and moaned, and vowed never to eat another wife again.

And Imarasugssuaq never did eat another wife. For Kalakav-siq's three brothers heard about what he had tried to do to their sister. They came to his hut and killed him. And ate him.

The Fox-Wife and the Penis of the Lake

A MAN AND HIS WIFE—they lived quite alone. Summers the man would venture out in his kayak and hunt for long periods of time. Once, when he returned, his wife was not there. Then it happened again and again; the wife would come back only after the husband. So one day the man pretended to go off hunting, but instead he followed his wife. He followed her all the way to a certain lake. She waded into the lake, saying: "Penis! Penis! Penis!" And then a huge penis emerged and she coupled with it so wildly that the water churned in the lake.

Now the man felt the greatest anger at his wife. It wasn't long before he went back to the lake by himself and there he shouted: "Penis! Penis! Penis!" At which the penis again appeared. The man beat it to death and cut it into small pieces. Then he came home and proceeded to throw these penis-pieces into the meat-pot. After they were cooked, he roused his wife: "Supper's ready . . ." The wife began to eat. "Umm, what's this that tastes so good?" she said. "It's your lover," he replied. "My lover?" "Yes. The penis of the lake." And the woman let out a moan and lay down on the ground, pulling her sleeping skins over her head.

But the man wasn't finished with his wife yet. As she lay there on the ground, he went out and gathered flies, maggots, and worms. These he placed beneath her sleeping skins. The creatures soon devoured her. And when there was nothing left of her, he set a fire and burned them to death, too.

Now the man was all by himself. But once he came back from a hunting trip and there was meat steaming in the pot. His *kamiks* had been mended and stockings put into them, as in his married days. The same thing happened again and again. Then one day, instead of leaving, the man hid in a crevice in the ice. And soon he saw a little she-fox, quite pretty, standing at his meat-pot. "What are you doing here?" he asked. She didn't say a thing, she just continued to stir the meat. Whereupon he leaped on her and made her his wife. She was a better wife than the last, for she would wait patiently for him while he was out hunting.

Then it happened that the two of them set out for winter quarters. On their way they visited another married couple, a piece of shit and a rabbit, man and wife. And with this couple they decided to stay for the rest of the winter. Soon they had exchanged wives. The man lay with the rabbit while the piece of shit lay with the she-fox. This did not work out very well, as all of a sudden the fox exclaimed: "This place smells of shit!" And the shit replied: "Whew, fox stench!" The fox, upon hearing this, slipped through a little hole in the doorskin and was gone. The man began to have harsh words with the shit. "You have driven my wife away," he said. "Well, if you want her, why don't you go after her?" the shit told him.

So the man followed his wife's tracks in the snow. On one side they were the footprints of a human being, and on the other the tracks of a fox. He followed them right up to a small dark cave. He figured that she had gone into the cave. So he called to her to come out. And then out of the cave came a creature that was half-human and half-fly, saying: "I'll be your wife. Take me! Take me!" When the man said no, it went back in again. Then the man called out once more for his wife. And now it was a she-maggot that came out, and it said: "Take me! Take me!" But the man would not have her, either. And he entered the cave himself, to retrieve his wife. Inside there was only a worm. This worm said to him: "You are a man who must suffer because of what you did to me..."

Fly, maggot, and worm—they were all creatures whom he had destroyed. And now the man knew that he was alone, quite alone, forever.

Blubber Boy

ONCE THERE WAS A girl whose boyfriend drowned in the sea. Her parents could do nothing to console her. Nor did any of the other suitors interest her—she wanted the fellow who drowned and no one else. Finally she took a chunk of blubber and carved it into the shape of her drowned boyfriend. Then she carved the boyfriend's face. It was a perfect likeness.

"Oh, if only he were real!" she thought.

She rubbed the blubber against her genitals, round and round, and suddenly it came alive. Her handsome boyfriend was standing in front of her. How delighted she was! She presented him to her parents, saying:

"As you can see, he didn't drown, after all..."

The girl's father gave his daughter permission to marry. Now she went with her blubber boy to a small hut just outside the village. Sometimes it would get very warm inside this hut. And then the blubber boy would start to get quite weary. At which point he would say: "Rub me, dear." And the girl would rub his entire body against her genitals. This would revive him.

One day the blubber boy was hunting harbor seals and the sun beat down on him harshly. As he paddled his kayak home, he started to sweat. And as he sweated, he got smaller. Half of him had melted away by the time he reached the shore. Then he stepped out of the kayak and fell to the ground, a mere pile of blubber.

"What a pity," said the girl's parents. "And he was such a nice young man, too..."

The girl buried the blubber beneath a pile of stones. Then she went into mourning. She plugged up her left nostril. She did not sew. She ate neither the eggs of sea-birds nor walrus meat. Each day she visited the blubber in its grave and talked to it and as she did so, walked around the grave three times in the direction of the sun.

After the period of mourning, the girl took another chunk of blubber and began carving again. Again she carved it into the shape of her drowned boyfriend and again rubbed the finished product against her genitals. Suddenly her boyfriend was standing beside her, saying, "Rub me again, dear..."

Uutaaq, The Hunter

THERE WAS A young man named Uutaaq who by accident swallowed the spear-point of his harpoon. This gave him some pain, poking away at his innards. He broke wind against a herd of narwhals. The spear-point shot out of his ass and flew through each heart of each and every narwhal in the herd. Uutaaq was acclaimed the greatest hunter in the world. He had his choice of women for the rest of his days.

Counting Hairs

THERE WERE ONCE two brothers who were hunters. The one had just killed a reindeer, and the other had a big seal in his sledge. They met as they were heading home one evening, and they fell to talking. At last the first brother said:

"Not to make light of your catch, but everyone knows that a reindeer pelt has more hairs than a seal pelt."

"Oh no," said the other, "a seal pelt has more hairs."

"A reindeer pelt has more..."

"Everyone knows that a seal pelt has more..."

And so they sat down on the snow and the brother with the seal began to count its hairs, pulling them out one by one. The brother with the reindeer did likewise. Days passed, blizzards came, the fjord froze over. And still neither man would give in. Indeed, both of them sat there and counted hairs until they starved to death.

Utsuuq

ONCE THERE WAS A rather awkward hunter whose penis got tangled up in his harpoon line. He caught a seal and the seal gave a rough pull and the man felt all his strength leave his body. But he decided to make the best of it. He went home and put on woman's clothing. Now he called himself Utsuuq, Vagina, and announced that he was in need of a husband.

"You fool," said his mother. "You're a man, not a woman. You should be wearing man's clothing. And if you don't stop talking about a husband, I'm going to throw you out of the house."

This made Utsuuq quite angry, so he used magic and laid bare the skin from his entire body. When his mother looked at the skeleton that once had been her son, she dropped dead at once.

Now Utsuuq started to behave like a woman. He would not hunt. He bound his hair in a chignon and wore a *kapataq* over it. He softened fox skins with his teeth. And he drew little tattoos all over his arms and thighs. Monthly he made cuts at his groin so that he would bleed there.

Then it happened that a woman loaned her husband to Utsuuq for the night. The man was a big brawny type who would make a fine lover. But when Utsuuq removed his woman's clothing, the man saw that he was no woman. He said: "You are a *Tuneq*. Or some sort of madman. I will not sleep with you." At that Utsuuq again laid bare the skin from his body. His skeleton was so frightful that the man fell dead on the spot.

A while later Utsuuq decided to adopt a child. There was an orphan whom no one else would have, so the boy went to live with Utsuuq. And Utsuuq cared for him as though he were the boy's own mother. But one day the boy demanded some blubber.

"I have no blubber," Utsuuq said, "for I am a woman and do not hunt. Find some man if you want to chew on blubber."

"But you are a man," the orphan said. "I have often seen you when you go out to take a piss and you piss like a man."

Utsuuq did not want to hear this sort of thing. Once again he laid bare the skin of his body. But the child was not at all frightened by Utsuuq's skeleton. He thought that it was only a plaything and ran his fingers over the ribs and eyeholes. Then Utsuuq was forced to use stronger magic. He reached into his chest and pulled out all of his entrails and placed them in a pile on the ground. "There!" he exclaimed. "Isn't that horrible?"

The child did not find Utsuuq's entrails horrible. But there were some dogs sniffing around the tent and they found them very interesting. These dogs came in and dragged off the whole lot.

"Stop!" shouted Utsuuq. "Those belong to me." And he chased the dogs all through the village. He was able to retrieve all of his entrails, which he put back in his body. All but the heart. One of the dogs had already eaten that. And without a heart, a person is nothing. Soon Utsuuq wasted away and died. He was buried beneath a pile of stones quite a distance from his fellow human beings.

The Sisters Who Married *Erqigdlit*

TWO SISTERS WENT OUT with their younger brother to collect berries. The boy was left behind in the boat while the girls gathered the berries. When they came back, they discovered that the little boy had fallen into the water and drowned. One of the sisters said:

"Our parents will kill us if they find out that we let Little Brother drown."

"This is so," replied the other. "We must run away from them forever."

And so the girls fled inland and they did not stop running until they came to where lived the *Erqigdlit*, the Dog-Headed People. Here they remained, quite a distance from their parents. They were looked after very nicely, and always had more than enough to eat. It wasn't long before each sister had married a dog-headed man.

In time the elder sister gave birth to a dog-headed child.

"So sweet," said her husband's mother, "but it would be better if you did not look at it just now."

And so the girl closed her eyes whenever she suckled the infant.

A while later she bore a son who had a human head, She named him after her drowned brother. His father, however, closed his eyes rather than look at the little boy.

The other sister gave birth to two children as well—one dog-headed, the other human.

Now the elder sister went with her husband to summer quarters on top of a *nunatak*. The younger remained at home chewing leather. She noticed that her husband seemed overly fond of feeding her musk ox haunch. In the fall, they met and began to chat.

The younger sister said:

"Do you know that they are planning to kill us?"

"No!"

"It is so. I overheard my husband's mother talking to your husband's mother. She said, 'I can't wait till these Human Beings get fat so that we can eat them.'"

At that the girls decided to run away again. The elder sister went back to her dog-headed child and killed it and hung it on the wall with her husband's harpoon line. She put the other child in an *amaut* on her back. The younger sister did the same thing with her children, killing the dog-headed one, keeping the other.

Now the sisters were running over the hills. Although the snow was thick, they ran very fast. Behind them they could hear a terrible barking. It was the Dog-Headed People pursuing them.

All at once the younger sister stopped and said: "We are running too fast. Our poor children will strangle."

Replied her sister: "*Ajornaarmat.* Such is life. Better that they strangle than that we end up in the cooking pot."

In fact, both children strangled shortly after that. The sisters took them from their *amauts* and flung them away, weeping bitterly. However, it was much easier to run now.

At last they arrived at their old home. Their parents did not kill them because of their brother. Indeed, there was another little brother now.

"Get ready to leave right away," the sisters told their parents, "or the *Erqigdlit* will kill us and eat us all."

And just as they climbed into their *umiaq*, they heard the loud barking of dogs. The *Erqigdlit* came into view and rushed down to the shore and barked at them to come back. The elder sister burst into tears when she saw her husband, for she remembered that he'd been rather kind to her. The same with the younger sister. Her husband had been an excellent lover. But they did not go back.

"Better loneliness than the cooking pot," their father observed.

For fear of the *Erqigdlit*, parents and children settled on an island far from the coast. At length both girls married again and gave birth to normal children. But they always felt sad, in spite of all, about leaving their dog-headed husbands.

The Ghost That Ate Children

ONCE UPON A TIME there was a woman whose husband was in the habit of beating her. If he was angry with his dogs, he would beat her. If he was angry with the weather, he would beat her. And if there were no seals, he would beat her. She told him:

"If you beat me one more time, I'm going to run away."

And he beat her for saying this. So she took their little child and wandered off down the coast. She had not wandered very far when she came to an old ruined house near the edge of a cliff. The woman decided that they would spend the night there. But in the middle of the night, she heard a voice saying:

"Ah, a tasty little child for me to eat..."

The woman asked whose voice this was. Came the reply:

"I am the ghost of a man who once starved to death here."

And now there emerged a big bloated shape from out of the walls. Huge hands grabbed the child and took it back into the walls. Soon the woman heard the crunching of bones.

"Oh, my child! My poor child!"

But the child was no more. The house was once again silent. Weeping, the woman ran out along the cliffs and did not stop running until she reached home. She told her husband that a ghost had just eaten their child. He replied:

"This time I'm not going to beat you. Instead I'm going to kill you. Because I know that you ate our child yourself."

"First come with me to this house," she told him, "then you can kill me afterwards."

And so they climbed along the cliffs to the house and there they waited for night to come. The man began to think of his dead child and all at once he started crying. Crying, in fact, like a child

himself. There came a voice from the back of the house: "Ah, a
tasty little child to eat..."

Then a huge bloated creature came out, its eyes popping from
its skull. Its hand reached out for the man, but he had a knife and a
spear with him and his wife also had a knife. Together they
stabbed and stabbed away at the creature. They could hear it
groaning in pain. Suddenly they could hear all the children that it
had devoured crying in its belly. They could hear their own child,
too. Then all was silence. The creature collapsed dead on the
ground and once again it became the body of the man who'd
starved to death.

Now the man and the woman went back home. From then on
the man never beat his wife again. And at length she gave birth to
another little child, who was never eaten by a ghost or anything
else.

Evat

POOR EVAT! His wife bore him seven children, all girls. One after the other, he threw them outside. One after the other, they froze or were eaten by dogs. Then his wife bore him a little son. Evat was delighted. *Aja*, quite delighted! But in the first week of his life the boy grew antlers like a reindeer and flippers like a seal, not to mention a codfish face. Evat threw his little son outside too.

The Two Women Who Found Freedom

ONCE THERE LIVED a man who had two wives. His name was Eqqorsuaq. And he was so jealous of these wives that he would keep them locked up in his hut. He would thrash them if they did not behave themselves. Or he would thrash anyone who happened to lay eyes on them. He killed a man named Angaguaq because rumor had it that Angaguaq had slept with one of the wives. Which he hadn't done. Eqqorsuaq was a somewhat mean-spirited person.

Finally the two women got a bit tired of their husband. They left him and fled along the coast until they were all worn out and hungry. When they could go no further, they saw the huge carcass of a whale washed up on a beach. They crawled in through the mouth and hid inside this carcass. The smell was foul, but better a foul smell than another thrashing.

Now Eqqorsuaq was in a furor. He searched high and low for his wives. He questioned everyone in the village and threatened not a few. But no one seemed to know about the missing women. At last the man paid a visit to the local *angakok*, who told him:

"You must look for the body of a big whale which is on the Skerry of the Heart-Shaped Mountain."

And so Eqqorsuaq set out for the Skerry of the Heart-Shaped Mountain. He sang old drum-songs all along the way, for he looked forward to the pleasure of thrashing his wives. At last he arrived at his destination and saw the dead whale. But the stench was so awful that he could get nowhere near it. He called out again and again for the women, yet there came no answer. Perhaps they were no longer here. Eqqorsuaq camped on the beach for three days and then went home, determined to thrash the *angakok*.

Meanwhile the two wives lived on inside the whale. They had grown so accustomed to the stench that it did not bother them. They had plenty of food to eat, however rotten, and a warm place to sleep. It is said that they were very happy in their new home.

Konjujuk's Friend

A BOY NAMED Konjujuk had neither parents, relations, nor friends. And so he was abused by everyone. He was chained like a dog to the house-passage. People gave him only certain scraps of food which they would not eat themselves. Or they would toss him bones with barely any meat at all. If Konjujuk complained that he was hungry, they would thrash him with a sealskin scourge.

One night the boy was looking up at the sky and it seemed to him that the moon had a face. As there was no one else, he called out to this face for help. Right away the Man in the Moon came down and, like all the others, proceeded to beat poor Konjujuk. He used a scourge with small stones tied into it. The more the boy cried, the harder the Man in the Moon beat him. After a while, the Man said:

"Now you are strong enough to take care of yourself."

And he returned to his home in the moon.

Konjujuk broke the chains which held him. He found that he was able to pick up an *umiaq* and twirl it about using only one hand. He also found that he could topple heavy boulders into the sea. He was busy doing this when along came two men who were in the habit of thrashing him.

"There's Konjujuk," they said. "Let's give him another beating. If he survives it, we'll reward him with a piece of rancid reindeer liver..."

As they raised fists against him, Konjujuk crashed their heads together so that their brains leaked out their ears.

Then another man tried to put the boy back into his chains. Konjujuk merely wrapped his chain around this man's neck until he started to choke. "Don't strangle me, you fool," the man gasped.

"All right, I won't strangle you," Konjujuk said. And he picked up the fellow and threw him over a cliff into the sea.

Now everyone else cowered in his hut for fear of the boy. But Konjujuk had had enough of human company. He walked into the mountains. He only stopped when he came to a range of mountains on the edge of the Inland Ice. Here, in a cave, he lived as a *qiviktoq*. If he saw a reindeer, he would leap on it and beat it to death. He could also beat a musk ox to death by drumming on its head with his hands. Indeed, Konjujuk was never lacking in food again. Nor did he ever again have to suffer anyone's abuse. He lived a pleasant sort of life in his cave. All thanks to his friend the Man in the Moon.

Terqilik and His Sons

THIS HAPPENED WHEN there was very little food in the world. A man named Terqilik had three sons and a wife who was pregnant. While the sons were out watching seal breathing holes, Terqilik became very hungry. So he killed his wife, flensed her and cooked her meat. The sons returned home and sniffed this meat and then realized that it belonged to their mother. But they were very hungry as well and thus not a word passed among them. They ate their mother.

Now Terqilik and his sons were without food again. They took to eating the lichen off rocks and *kamik* leather. One day the sons could not even find any breathing holes in the ice. They went back thinking that they would surely die now. And when they came into the house-passage, they smelled some meat cooking. One of the sons tasted this meat and said: "It tastes like father..."

And then appeared the ghost of their mother. She told them that she had frightened Terqilik to death and flensed him just as he had done to her. She said: "You must eat both your parents, my sons, if you wish to stay alive..."

And so the sons ate their father, too. Shortly after that, seals returned to the sea in large numbers. The sons never again had to eat any of their own kin. They grew up to be strong, healthy men.

Katiak

THERE WAS A GIRL named Katiak who would not marry. Men came from quite far away, but she refused them all. Then there arrived a very handsome man and he proved that he was an excellent hunter by spearing a bearded seal just outside Katiak's parents' house. Katiak decided to marry him. At last! sighed her parents.

Hardly had man and wife left the house when the man took off his clothing and put on a coat of thick white fur. Now Katiak could see that she had married an ice-bear. She tried to get away, but he clutched her tightly in his jaws. And he dragged her over the ice-floes, farther and farther from her home.

"Where are you taking me?" Katiak asked.

But when the bear opened his mouth to reply, the girl dropped out. She fell through the ice and into the sea and she did not stop sinking until she reached bottom. At the very bottom of the sea, everything was dark except for a tiny speck of light in the distance. Katiak decided to head toward this light. Soon all the creatures of the sea—fish, snails, and crabs—were tearing the flesh from her body. Piece by piece she was being eaten. In the end, only her bones remained. Even so she continued to walk toward the light. She walked right up onto dry land. Then she fell into a deep sleep.

Now Katiak was awake again. She was inside an ice-hut with a big stone lamp in the middle of the floor. There was a pile of meat beside her. Suddenly she was overcome by hunger. As soon as she would eat up the meat, a new pile would appear. And no matter how much she ate, she remained a skeleton. Nothing would cling to her bones. And no man would look at her—she would venture onto the ice and wave at the hunters, but they would flee from her, saying: "*Aja*, Skeleton, get away from me!"

But there was an *angakok* who happened to be father of some of these hunters. He said: "I will seek out this fearful skeleton. Perhaps it is someone whom I once knew."

And so the old man paid a visit to Katiak. He went into her ice-hut and there he saw the skeleton bent over, weeping mournfully. He thought: There is but one thing I can do... He began to beat a large drum, chanting:

"Flesh, flesh, flesh..."

And as he did this, flesh began to appear on Katiak's bones. The old man was quite surprised to see a pretty young woman take shape before him. In fact, he was so surprised that he went on beating the drum and singing: "Flesh, flesh, flesh..." As a result, he became young again himself. His own flesh lost all its wrinkles and his eyes became clear. Now he took the girl to wife.

That is how Katiak, who refused all suitors, found a husband.

Oherdluq, The Murderer

THIS OHERDLUQ WOULD invite people to come and live with him as his guests, and then he would kill them. No one escaped his hut alive. Young and old, healthy and unhealthy, he killed them all. There was an old woman, blind, deaf, and full of the burning sickness. He killed her as well, and threw her body into the sea.

"My husband is the best murderer in all the North," Oherdluq's wife would often brag.

Finally some men gathered together in order to put an end to Oherdluq. Two or three murders were understandable, but he had wiped out whole villages. Dozens of children were fatherless because of him. And dozens of fathers had children whom Oherdluq had thrown into the sea. It was time that he should suffer the same fate as his many victims.

The men journeyed to his hut. Oherdluq laughed when he saw them, even though they were all armed with arrows and harpoons. He was quite pleased that he would have so many people to kill all at once. It was just like a big feast. Indeed, Oherdluq killed them all in almost no time. The only wound he received was an arrow in the thigh. This his wife dressed and treated. Such a wound was a small price to pay, he thought, for so much fun.

Not long after this battle, a young woman arrived at his hut. Oherdluq thought about murdering her, but decided she would be more useful to him alive. She could help his wife take care of him. Perhaps she might even know a charm or two that could cure his wound. So he welcomed her handsomely, with a reindeer haunch over which he poured gruel from the bottom of a walrus's stomach.

Poor Oherdluq! He didn't realize that this woman had been sent by his enemies to do away with him. For she was menstruating. And a menstruating woman, if she comes in contact with a wound, is worse than the worst scourge.

The woman stayed for several days and all the while Oherdluq's condition grew worse. First he could not get up from his sleeping platform. Then he could hardly breathe. He was visited by the ghosts of all the people whom he'd killed. Each came in his turn, and accused him of doing evil for its own sake. At last his wound took over the rest of his body and he died.

The unclean woman had succeeded where arrows and harpoons had failed. Such are the ways of the world.

Pavia, Who Made Friends With a Stone

ONCE THERE LIVED a man named Pavia. No one liked this Pavia because he was dimwitted and hobbled about on all fours. In addition, he was an orphan. He would not be invited to dances or anything of that sort. Nor would any woman give him so much as a look.

The whole village decided to go away on a narwhal hunt. "Take me with you, take me with you," Pavia pleaded with the headman. For he was fearful that he would be attacked by ghosts if he were left behind. They left him behind anyway. A person like him was considered very bad luck on a whale hunt.

The first few days Pavia amused himself by singing and beating his drum. Then he grew very lonely. His eyes were drawn to a stone lying on the beach. He spoke to this stone: "You are all alone, like me. Come back with me to my house." And although the stone was quite heavy, he dragged it back to his house and placed it over his door.

"Friend Stone," he said, "if a ghost comes, fall down and kill him."

One night there was an awful odor which grew stronger with each passing minute. It smelled like rotten flesh suddenly being aired. Then Pavia heard these words: "Ah, nice blood to suck in this house..."

At the door there appeared a monstrous head, all swollen and greeny, ten times the size of a normal human head. A huge tongue licked huge lips. As the ghost entered, however, the stone fell down and killed him.

Now Pavia cut the ghost into pieces and put these pieces into all the stewpots in the village. Shortly after that, the people came back. They had not caught any whales. And here was Pavia capering around and beating his drum. This put them in a rather foul mood. One of the men struck Pavia, saying:

"You *seqijuk*! You good-for-nothing! It's your fault we didn't harpoon any whales. Why don't you jump off the cliffs into the sea?"

To which Pavia replied: "That's a fine thing to say when I've put meat in all your pots."

The villagers soon found out that this was true. Thus they had a big feast in which they ate the meat. And as each person chewed and swallowed it, he dropped dead. For (as even a half-wit knows) ghost meat is the most poisonous of all meats.

Now Pavia went back to his house and beat his drum. No doubt he lives there even today, singing and beating his drum and talking to his stone.

Arnatsiq

LONG AGO A man married a beautiful young woman named Arnatsiq. All went well with them until the man observed his wife pissing through her hands. She had two little vaginas in her palms. Then the man knew: His Arnatsiq was a *Tunit* whose real home was among ghosts deep inside the Earth. And so he strapped her to his kayak and took her far from his home place. There he deposited her on an ice-floe. For years Arnatsiq could be heard wandering about on the ice, sobbing: "My husband will not have me because I piss through my hands! My husband will not have me because I piss through my hands!" On certain nights, you can hear her sobbing still.

The Jealous Husband

THERE WAS A MAN who was always jealous of his wife. He watched her with the eyes of a raven. He would hide her *kamiks* whenever he went hunting so that she would not be able to go out herself. She was a prisoner in her own home. Nor did he ever exchange her with anyone else's wife, not even for a night. People thought him a rather selfish fellow.

The worst of it was that the man would stab his wife with a flensing knife every time he suspected her of being unfaithful. He would stab her in the chest, arms, and legs. After a while, she had so many scars that she appeared to be tattooed. She would cry out for him to stop torturing her, but he wouldn't. Rather, he would tell her:

"You must suffer because you've slept with such-and-such a hunter..."

But she had not slept with such-and-such a hunter, only with him.

Once, after one of these stabbings, the woman took to the cliffs. She had had enough of her jealous husband. Now she ran until she came to a place called Itivdlerssuaq, where a great *angakok* lived. And why do you have so many wounds on your body? the *angakok* inquired. She told him and pleaded with him to come to her aid.

"*Aja,*" he said, "I will fashion a *tupilak* who'll suck all the bones from your dear husband's body."

And this is what happened: The husband was furious with his wife, thinking that she had again run off with some hunter. He was waiting for her to come home so that he could stab her all the more vigorously. Suddenly there appeared a Being that was all mouth and stomach, with little scraggly limbs. It sucked at the husband's hands and one by one the fingerbones disappeared. Then it sucked at his ribs and they went, too. Then went his backbone and skull. At last there was nothing left of him but flabby skin lying on the ground. There it lay for quite some time, gathering maggots. Then somebody came in and saw it, and exclaimed:

"Whew! Why would anyone want to keep such a smelly old pelt?"

And he buried this smelly old pelt in a place where only dead dogs were buried.

Thus the wife got her revenge.

Girl of Stone

A GIRL NAMED Kala stood on a lonely headland and she saw two men in a kayak paddling toward her. One of the men shouted that he had no wife. Would she like to lie with him? But she had no interest in him, or the other one, so she told them to paddle on their way or they would taste her spear-point. And as she turned her back to them, she felt her hands and legs become stone. She called out:

"Kayak men, come back. You may take me to wife if you wish."

The kayak men paddled on. Now Kala felt her shoulders and head grow stiff. She called out again:

"Kayak men, dear kayak men. Please take me to wife."

Again they ignored her. Now all but her navel had turned to stone.

"Dear kayak men, you may *both* take me..."

Too late! She was now a pillar of stone. For the Stone Spirit had married her as it marries anyone who turns his back on his fellow human beings.

Forever more Kala remained on that headland. She did not have offspring. Sea-birds came and shat upon her.

The Woman Who Married Her Son's Wife

ONCE THERE LIVED an old woman who desired her son's pretty young wife. This son was a hunter who often would be gone for many days at a time. Once, while he was gone, the old woman sat down and made herself a penis out of sealbone and skins. She fastened this penis to her waist and showed it to her daughter-in-law, who exclaimed: "How nice..." Then they slept together. Soon the old woman was going out to hunt in a big skin kayak, just like her son. And when she came back, she would take off her clothes and move her breasts up and down, saying: "Sleep with me, my dear little wife. Sleep with me..."

It happened that the son returned from his hunting and saw his mother's seals lying in front of the house. "Whose seals are these?" he asked of his wife.

"None of your business," she replied.

Being suspicious of her, he dug a hole behind their house and hid there. He figured that some hunter was claiming his wife in his absence. Soon, however, he saw his mother paddling home in her kayak with a big hooded seal. Mother and son never caught anything but big hooded seals. The old woman reached land and took off her clothes, then moved her breasts up and down, saying: "My sweet little wife, kindly delouse me..."

The son was not pleased by his mother's behavior. He came out of hiding and struck the old woman so hard that he killed her. "Now," he said to his wife, "You must come away with me because our home place has a curse on it."

The wife began to quiver and shake all over. "You've killed my dear husband," she cried. And would not stop crying.

All at once the son saw his mother's penis, very worn at the tip. Now he had no choice but to strike his wife dead, too. He buried her in the same grave as his mother. Then he went away and built a new house a great distance from the old one. And there he sits to this day, happily delousing himself.

Tugtutsiak

TUGTUTSIAK WAS A bachelor whose old mother was always chiding him about not taking a wife. Finally he set out in search of a suitable woman. He paddled for three days and then came to an island where three brothers lived with their sister. Unfortunately, the brothers told him that they would never give their sister in marriage because she looked after them so well. So Tugtutsiak paddled off to another island, where there was a young woman living with her mother. Unfortunately, she refused him because it was foretold that she would marry a man with a large birthmark on his neck. He went to another island and courted a woman there, but soon learned that she was a bitch-dog under an enchantment. So now he went to an island of only women—all young, healthy, and fat. But none of them would have him, for they said he was too old. As he was leaving this last place, he saw a woman on the cliff waving and gesturing to him. He paddled over and put his arms around her, but he soon discovered that she was only a rock. Well, Tugtutsiak decided to marry that rock. He placed it on his kayak and brought it back home with him. It is said that they had a very nice life together.

The Man Who Was a Mother

A MAN AND A WOMAN could not get any children. This made them very unhappy as well as the butt of quite a few jokes. At last a visitor from the South told them about a female *angakok* who might be able to help them. Having been struck by lightning, she had certain gifts. The man clapped his hands. He said goodbye to his wife and climbed into his kayak and paddled toward Cape Farewell. After some weeks, he came to the little island where the old woman lived. Yes, she said, she might be able to help him. Then she reached into her tunic and brought out two dried fish, a male and a female. He was to present his wife with the male if he wanted a boy-child and the female if he wanted a girl-child. The man clapped his hands again. He hopped into his kayak and paddled toward home as fast as he could. But it wasn't long before he grew hungry from so much paddling. He gazed at the two fish. "What matter," he thought, "if I eat the female. It is a son we want..." And so he ate the female fish. Soon he was feeling a bit uncomfortable. And after some weeks, his belly started to swell. By the time he arrived home, he could hardly squeeze out of his kayak. His wife tended him night and day. Then one morning he gave birth to a healthy baby girl. Man and woman clapped their hands. They were delighted with their little daughter: What matter if her father was her mother?

Four Wives

THERE WAS A pregnant woman whose husband was killed by a group of *Tunit*. They drilled holes in his knees and sucked out all his juices. On the very same day of this murder the woman gave birth to a son. The boy grew up very quickly. His mother made him strong by pulling at the knuckles of his hands and feet. He went out in his father's kayak when he was two years old. When he was three, he killed his first seal. And soon he was hitting his head against the wallskins because he didn't have a wife.

"But you are only a child," his mother said.

"I am child and man both."

And so the mother set out with the boy in search of a wife. They traveled for some time without seeing anything suitable. Finally they headed inland and came to a village of the Dog-Headed People. By now the boy needed a wife rather badly and was not too concerned about the shape of her head.

"A wife for my son!" the mother called out.

The people laughed and told her that her son ought to have a little doll to play with instead of a wife. But they gave him a dog-headed woman to marry. She was very attractive (except for her head). And she seemed to have a decent enough temperament. First night together, however, she tried to eat his genitals. He killed her.

Then the mother went with her son to another place. Here all the women were taken except for one. She had fingernails longer than a harpoon. First night in bed she kept scraping his back. She said she liked nothing better than to scrape the skin off a man's back. When she finished with the back, she started in with the chest and thighs. Thus she had made skeletons out of many men.

The boy killed her, too.

By this time the mother was getting old and feeble. She informed her son that he would have to continue his journey alone. Then she walked off a cliff.

And so her son went on by himself in search of a wife. He arrived at a village where there seemed to be an abundance of women. He had his pick. And chose a fine-looking woman with long blue-black hair tied tight in a bun. She could clean a sealskin as rapidly as any woman and her hands were nice and fat.

Husband and wife got along very well until he realized that she was barren. Then he kicked her and beat her and dragged her around the house by her hair. At last he threw her into the sea. The rest of the village was furious, for it was a place where the killing of barren women was no longer tolerated. As punishment, he was forced to marry a woman whom no one else would take. She never said a word. She could not mend *kamiks*. Her eyes had not a single bit of sparkle in them. She was boring, boring, boring. And after a short while with her, the fellow went crying on the graves of his other wives.

Such is the life of man, my friends.

Nutik

THERE WAS A MAN named Nutik who would never let anyone see his face. Not even his own wife was allowed to see it. In the house, he would put out the lamps and they would eat in the dark. He would mount her only from behind, or with his face turned around almost to the back. But he was an excellent hunter and always brought home game, which mattered more than good looks.

One day Nutik came in and put out the lamps, as was his custom. Then they began to eat supper. His mother-in-law said to his wife:

"Why must we always eat in the dark? Is it because your husband is in the habit of eating his own shit?"

Nutik was so upset by this that he lit the lamps and at last showed his face. It was nothing but cracks. He took off his clothes. His body was nothing but a mass of cracks, too. "I do not belong among the human beings," he said. And he walked out into the night completely naked. He walked until he found an iceberg, then jumped onto it. For Nutik was in truth only cracks in the ice disguised as a human being and now he was going back to his real home.

His wife turned into a she-fox and his mother-in-law turned into a dog, always sniffing at one midden heap or another. Friend Nutik was the luckiest of the lot, neither hungry nor homeless, just sitting on his nice iceberg and peering out at the sea.

Mikisoq and The Skull

THERE WAS A WOMAN named Mikisoq who had her own ideas about men. Many men wanted to marry her, but she refused them all. None of them, she thought, was worth more than two knobs of rabbit shit. Then one night a large skull rolled into her hut and turned into a man. She led this man to her sleeping platform and they coupled wildly. Next morning, he was a skull again. So it always happened: skull, man, and skull again.

Now Mikisoq was hungry. The skull grinned. And by nightfall there was a bearded seal lying by the door.

Now she wanted some *mataq*. And soon there was a slab of *mataq* in her meat tub. Mikisoq was so pleased that she kissed and hugged her lover, saying: "*Ai*, you are a quite wonderful skull..."

One day he brought her the biggest reindeer haunch she'd ever seen. Another day, a nice fat walrus—enough to feed a family for a month. In the end, Mikisoq married the skull. And never again did she suffer from want of food.

The Luckless Hunter

ONCE THERE WAS A man named Kiniqsaluq who was just like any other man, perhaps even better looking, except that he was a very unlucky hunter. He would sit by a seal's breathing hole for days and nothing would happen. When others would come back with game, he would bring back only a few small codfish or even smaller capelin. Or when others brought back a brace of ptarmigans, he could manage only insects.

Now this Kiniqsaluq fell in love with a girl named Akpuqtuq. The two of them would have gotten married if it wasn't for the girl's father. He was an old man who could no longer provide for himself. He wanted a decent hunter in the family. A hunter who could bring in seals rather than put a curse on them. And Kiniqsaluq seemed to put a curse on all game. The old man said to his daughter: "Better to marry your wiping moss than marry that fool..."

And so Kiniqsaluq and Akpuqtuq decided that they would run away together. They would do this at night after the girl had slipped her father a strong sleeping potion.

Now the appointed night came and Kiniqsaluq approached the hut. He entered it. The lamp was burning low, but he could see the girl and her father wrapped up in their sleeping skins. He grabbed the girl, sleeping skins and all, and dashed off with her. Soon he was making his way across an ice bridge that spanned a very deep gorge. Having crossed this bridge, he smashed it to pieces so that the father could not pursue them. Then he continued on, quite pleased with himself. Who says I'm so unlucky? he smiled.

Once he got to his own hut, Kiniqsaluq unwrapped the bundle

inside which slept Akpuqtuq. And, to his surprise, he found that he had picked up and carried off the girl's father instead of the girl herself. He hurried back, but the ice bridge was gone. There was a huge space that separated him from the other side. He would never have his Akpuqtuq now. Sadly he returned to his hut. The old man was awake and quite angry. He said: "Rid me of my lice, you fool." Kiniqsaluq did as he was told. And the two of them lived there together forever more, each picking lice from the other's body.

Nakasungnak, The Fool

THIS NAKASUNGNAK WAS a man who would never listen to what anyone told him. If someone said that a certain woman was in reality a ghost, he would hop into her sleeping skins right away. If he was told not to venture to a certain place for fear of an avalanche, he would go immediately and camp there for the night. It was said that his people had originated from the South, where men are foolish. It was also said that he had once entered his wife's womb so that she had become pregnant with her own husband—and being twice born, he was twice a fool.

One day the call was raised that an ice-bear had come to the neighborhood. Normally such an animal would be hunted, but word got around that this one was a *tupilak* in bear disguise. It would mean death for the person who killed it. Thus everyone dashed back to their huts. Not Nakasungnak. He ran in the opposite direction, toward the bear, armed with only his flensing knife. "Prepare to die, big fellow," he said to the bear, which simply opened its mouth and swallowed him up, flensing knife and all.

"Well, it's all over for Nakasungnak," remarked the headman of the village.

Now the bear started to walk away, but then it staggered and toppled to the ground. Everyone watched in astonishment as a knife emerged from between its ribs. The knife carved a hole out of which jumped Nakasungnak. He was unharmed. He waved the knife and said:

"Bear steaks, friends."

And the bear provided the village with food for quite some time.

Then summer came. There arose from the bogs an enormous

swarm of mosquitoes. The entire village headed indoors. Nakasungnak was warned to do likewise, else he would be in big
trouble. But he only laughed, saying:

"I will teach these silly little mosquitoes a lesson..."

And again he ran with his flensing knife in the opposite direction of everyone else. People saw him thrashing away at the
mosquitoes with his knife, yelling, "Die! Die!" And they they saw
him no more. That evening, when they came out of their huts,
they found only Nakasungnak's knife lying among the rocks. The
mosquitoes had eaten even the man's bones.

Two Men, One Kayak

TWO MEN AND A WOMAN lived together on an island. The men shared the woman, which was all right. But as they only had one kayak, they had to share it as well. Which was not all right. One of the men would always want to paddle away in search of game. They would get into terrible fights about the use of the kayak. Finally, after one of these fights, the elder man strapped the woman to his back and paddled off from the island.

"Don't leave me by myself!" the other man pleaded.

Shouted back the first: "I'll return in a year to see how you're doing."

The poor fellow had no means of getting food. For days he rummaged on the shore, eating shellfish and bits of sorrel. But it was not enough. "O Woman of the Sea," he said, "kindly send me real food or I'll starve." And behold! that very night the body of a big bow-headed whale washed up on the island. The man flensed away at it until he had enough blubber and meat to last him a whole winter. Now he was quite content. He even became a sort of *qivigtoq,* treasuring rocks and his own loneliness more than human company.

After the year had passed, his friend returned in the kayak. "Hey! Where are you?" he called out. But the other was hiding from him. And when the friend headed inland to search for him, he raced down to the shore and stole the kayak.

"Don't leave me! Don't leave me!"

"I'll come back in a year to see how you're doing," the man replied.

And being honorable, he did come back to the island. But all he found was the elder man's bones bleaching on the shore. It had been a bad year for whales.

Sermerssuaq

SERMERSSUAQ WAS SO powerful that she could lift a kayak on the tips of three fingers. She could kill a seal merely by drumming on its head with her fists. She could rip asunder a fox or hare. Once she arm-wrestled with Qasordlanguaq, another powerful woman, and beat her so easily that she said: "Poor Qasordlanguaq could not even beat one of her own lice at arm-wrestling." Most men she could beat and then she would tell them: "Where were you when the testicles were given out?" Sometimes this Sermerssuaq would show off her clitoris. It was so big that the skin of a fox would not fully cover it. *Aja*, and she was the mother of nine children, too!

The Iron-Tailed Woman

ONCE UPON A TIME a woman named Anninguaq had a tail of iron which she employed in the following manner: She would make love to a man until he fell asleep. Then she would jump up and down on him passionately, and gore him with her tail. No man ever survived a night with Anninguaq.

One day there came to her shack a brawny young hunter named Saqaq. He came from the North and was known for his ability to find seals when no one else could find them. Indeed, Saqaq untied several hooded seals from his bladder-float and brought them up to the shack.

"He must have a fine penis who is such a fine hunter," thought Anninguaq.

When she figured that he was asleep, she jumped up from her sleeping skins. And thrust herself down, tail first, as hard as she could. But Saqaq was not asleep and he simply moved over, with the result that the tip of her tail broke off. This did not please her.

"I think it's time for me to be going now," he said. And he went down to the shore and climbed into his kayak.

"Well, may your kayak sink to the bottom of the sea!" Anninguaq shouted after him.

And his kayak was almost sucked into a whirlpool which appeared as a result of her magic. He was only able to survive by employing a bit of magic of his own and singing the whirlpool into submission. After he escaped, he shouted back at Anninguaq:

"Nice try, but it didn't work. So now let it be your tail that sinks to the bottom of the sea . . ."

All of a sudden the tail broke off and rolled down into the water. It floated around for a brief while, then it sank from sight altogether. For Saqaq had some experience of women with tails and he knew how to recite the words that best worked against them.

After that Anninguaq never gored another man to death again.

Asalok's Family

THERE WAS A MAN named Asalok who lived all alone. He used to amuse himself that a bunch of seal-skulls were his children. He'd toss one of these skulls into the sea and exclaim: "Look! Your poor little brother is drowning." Or he'd stand them on the rocks and climb into his kayak, saying: "I'll be hungry when I get back, so cook me up some meat." And when there was no meat, he'd shout at them: "Bad children! Didn't I tell you to make my dinner?" But then he'd kiss each of the seal-skulls and tell them that he loved them all the same.

Once this Asalok happened to see some women bathing in a lake. When these women saw him, all of them changed into sea-gulls and flew away—all but one, whose clothing Asalok had taken.

"I want my clothes," the woman said. "If you will marry me," Asalok replied. And she agreed to marry him if he would give back her clothes, but he knew she would fly away just like her sisters, so he only gave her some maggoty old skins of his own. And then he led her home.

Now the woman became Asalok's wife. She cooked his meat and chewed leather for his *kamiks*. At length she bore him a son, and then another, and then a third. Asalok taught his sons how to hunt and fish. But the mother would take them to collect bird feathers and wings, saying: "Sweet little children, you are kin to the birds..."

One morning Asalok's family flew away. He was upset just like any other father, so he set out after them in his kayak. He paddled around the fjords, crying: "Children! Oh, my children!" Soon he met an old woman who told him that his family was living in an ice-hut on a nearby cliff. Then she changed into an eagle and flew away.

But the old eagle-woman was right, for there was an ice-hut on the cliff. Asalok peered in the window and saw his wife and children, along with a crowd of other people: they were sitting around and gaily chatting with each other. The man threw open the door and lo! the hut turned into a rookery and all the people became sea-gulls. Asalok found himself standing in a heap of turf and bird-shit. His wife looked at him with red angry eyes. His sons ignored him. And finally one by one they all flew away.

Then Asalok went back home to his seal-skulls.

Island of Women

IN THE TIME OF the forefathers, there was an island where all the men had died and only women were left alive. After a while, these women learned how to hunt and fish just like men. But they missed having men very much.

Once a man paddled his kayak to this island. The women went wild over him. They ran from their homes and embraced him so violently that he suffocated to death.

Another time a man came and so many women lay with him that his penis dropped off. He vowed that he would never come back again to the island of women.

At length the women were so eager for men that they married their own boy children. They slept with these children even though they were still in the *amaut*. And because the women lay on top, the little boys did not grow. Their mothers had taken all their strength from them.

—*Little man, little man, why will you not grow?*
—*Because I am child and husband both to my mother. I piss in my pants, and yet I have a beard.*
—*Little man, little man, can you not walk?*
—*Of course I can walk, but only inside the amaut on my mother's back.*
—*Little man, little man, why is that you're crying?*
—*Because babies are supposed to cry, that's why.*

There was no issue from these men. They grew old, their mothers grew old, all died. And the island of women became an island of no one. Which it remains to this very day.

The Slab of Meat

THIS HAPPENED IN THE famine times to a man named Kagungnaq. He had eaten his last bit of reindeer tallow and moss. Now he crouched at one seal breathing hole and then another. Now he searched the cliffs for auks. Now he found the tracks of musk-oxen, but he had no strength to follow them. And so he stumbled back home to die. But behold! there was a nice slab of meat lying on the floor of his hut. Quickly he made a fire and boiled some water. Then he flensed the meat, chopped it up, and threw it into the pot. "*Aja!*" he exclaimed, "Why do my eyes gaze at only darkness?" He died before he could eat the meat. For Kagungnaq had flensed and chopped up his own thigh, and thrown it into the stew-pot.

V. Animals

The Raven and the Seagull

A RAVEN AND A SEAGULL got into a fight over a piece of meat. The raven was on the Inuit's side, the seagull on the side of White Man. They fought for days, for weeks, even for months. Whoever won, his side would be the strongest. They tore and bit furiously at each other. At last the seagull won: White Man would be stronger and more plentiful than the Inuit. But by the time he flew away with the piece of meat, it had become quite rancid.

Whale's Wife

ONCE A WOMAN named Illitsina went out to collect some mussels on the beach. She was very pretty and many men fancied her. And while she was standing there on the beach, a whale also took a fancy to her and claimed her. Now Illitsina went to live with the whale, husband and wife, in the depths of the sea. As the whale was stronger, it was not her lot to object. In fact, she rather liked it. When the whale exchanged wives with a kayaker, she liked it much less. "More! More!" she exclaimed. The kayaker gave her back and never exchanged wives with a whale again. The same thing happened when the whale exchanged wives with a walrus, a musk-ox, and a bearded seal. Illitsina stayed with the whale until she died and then she was washed ashore at the very same beach where she had been collecting mussels long ago. No one recognized her, for she had long since taken on the shape of a whale. Her meat and blubber fed people for one whole winter.

The Mother's Skull

THERE WAS ONCE A pregnant woman who went searching for berries. Her name was Itsilik. Soon it began to rain, so Itsilik took refuge in a cave. She thought: I'll just stay here until the rain stops.

However, Itsilik was not alone in the cave. For it also happened to be the home of a she-bear. This bear took one look at Itsilik and decided that she would be a very tasty morsel. But as the bear proceeded to rip apart the woman's body, she found a boy-child in her womb. She kept the child and ate his mother.

Now the boy was raised by this bear-mother. He was taught to fish, to hunt game, and to dance on the ice-floes. The bear raised him like her own, yes, even better than her own. At night she would warm him against her body as though it were his own sleeping skins.

Once the boy saw some creatures who walked upright. He asked his mother what they were.

"Oh," she said, "they are nasty little human beings. And if you don't stay away from them, they will kill you."

Another time he found a skull in the cave. "Whose skull is this?" he said.

Replied the bear: "I really don't know..."

The skull became one of the boy's favorite playthings. He took it with him wherever he went. He slept with it cradled in his arms. He fingered its eyeholes fondly. He even played ball with it.

And now the skull began to talk to him. "Help me, my son!" Or: "I am your true mother..."

"Who are you talking to?" the bear would ask him.

"Oh, just this dirty old skull..."

One day the boy went to hunt hooded seals and he took the
skull along with him. He came upon a group of the creatures who
walked upright. They seemed a little surprised to see a naked boy
on the ice. They gazed at him and then realized that he had to be
Itsilik's son. The *angakok* said:

"Let me have a look at that skull..."

For a day and a night he muttered magical words and passed his
hands over the skull. Even as he was doing this the skull seemed
to acquire flesh. Suddenly it sprouted arms and legs. And at last it
became a full-grown woman, who turned out to be Itsilik herself.
Right away she grasped the boy to her breast. From then on
mother and son were able to live together as though nothing had
happened.

But the bear mourned her boy-child for the rest of her life.

"Spare My Life"

THERE WAS A LITTLE fly which happened to land on a boy's head. It was such a tiny thing that it didn't think anyone would notice. But then somebody said:

"Ugh, look at that nasty fly! Kill it!"

The fly could talk, but only the boy could hear what it said: "Spare my life, please spare my life! I have a grandson of my own at home and he will be very unhappy if I never come back."

Such a little creature, and a grandfather! The boy spared his life, and he flew toward home with many fond thoughts of mankind. However, he paused along the way on a man's nose. The man cursed the fly and slapped him dead and then crushed his body beneath his foot.

So much for fond thoughts of mankind.

The Raven and the Whale

THERE WAS ONCE A raven who by accident flew into the mouth of a big bow-headed whale. He flew right down the throat and ended up in the belly. There he saw a little house built of ribs and soft hides; a shabby little house, just like a human dwelling. Inside this house was a young woman minding a blubber lamp. "You may stay here as long as you like," she told him, "but you must never touch this lamp." For the lamp was the whale's heart.

The raven decided to stay there for quite awhile. The woman was very pleasant company. Likewise she did all the work. "Eat," she'd say, and offer him some fish, mussels, or crabs which the whale had swallowed. There would be more *mataq* than he could eat in a dozen lifetimes. Sometimes the raven would even sleep with the woman.

"Is there anything you would like?" the woman would ask him.

"Yes," said the raven. "I would like to touch the lamp."

"You must never, never touch the lamp," she told him.

But this made the raven all the more curious. More than anything else, he wanted to touch that lamp. He gazed at it for long hours. And once, while the woman's back was turned, he walked up and pecked at it. Instantly the lamp went out and the woman fell down dead.

Now the raven stumbled around in the dark. At last he found the throat-passage and crawled through it. Then he climbed on top of the whale, which was dead. He saw that they were floating toward a human village, so he turned himself into a man. "Behold!" he exclaimed, "I've just killed this enormous bow-headed whale without even using a harpoon..."

No one believed him. Perhaps he could show off his hunting

prowess once again? Whenever you wish, he declared. And he went to live in that village, waiting for the opportunity to show off his ability. Then one day a herd of narwhals was sighted in the harbor. "Leave this to me," he said. He got into a kayak and paddled it toward the herd. Almost at once the kayak was knocked over and he was pierced by a narwhal's horn. Thus did the mighty hunter die. But as he died, he turned back into a raven, and was eaten by one of the narwhals.

The Two Girls and Their Husbands

THERE WERE TWO GIRLS playing with bones which they found on the beach. One of them had eagle-bones, and the other had a bone from a whale. They were rubbing these bones happily all over their bodies.

"I'm going to have an eagle for my husband," said the first girl.

"You think that's so great," the other replied. "Well, I'm going to have a huge whale for *my* husband."

All at once an eagle appeared in the sky. And then a big whale swam up to the shore. The eagle flew down and carried off the first girl, while the whale grabbed the other in his mouth and dove with her to the bottom of the sea. Both girls had gotten what they asked for.

The eagle took his new wife to a tall sea-cliff. He put her in a warm little nest, from which she could not move, and brought her small auks for food. Each night he made love to her by grasping her and flapping his wings against her back. "Is there anything more you want, dearest?" he would ask. "Yes," she'd say, "I'd like you to return me to my own people." "Never," he told her.

But all the while the girl was taking the sinews from the small auks and making a rope out of them. At last the rope reached down to the sea. One day, when the eagle was off hunting, she saw a kayaker at the base of the cliff. And she went sliding down her rope until she landed in the water beside him. The kayaker fished her out and brought her home to her parents.

Now the eagle was furious when he discovered that his wife was gone. For he loved her perhaps more than he would have loved another eagle. He went to the village where the girl lived and flew over her father's house and demanded the return of his wife. Said the father: "I'll give her back if you can prove that you're worthy of her." "How can I do that?" the eagle said. Replied the father: "Let me have a look at your penis..." Whereupon the eagle spread his wings so that he could show his penis, of which he was rather proud. Then the father took an arrow and shot him directly in the heart. The eagle fell to the ground, dead.

As for the girl whom the whale had taken, she was tied to the bottom of the sea by a rope. By day her mate set her to work picking the lice from his body. By night she was forced to couple with him. He fed her sea-scorpions and small crabs. "Is there anything more you want, dearest?" he would ask her. "Yes," she said, "set me free." He refused to do this because he wouldn't be able to get anyone else to pick off his lice.

At last the girl chewed through the rope that bound her. Then she swam to the surface. The whale came after her, saying: "I'm going to beat you, dearest, because that's what one does to a wife who tries to run away." She threw her coat at him and he grabbed it and beat at it with his tail. For he thought she was inside it.

Now the girl was quite a distance ahead of him, and swimming toward land. The whale shouted after her: "For that little trick, I'm going to beat you even harder when I catch you. I'll make you look like rotten guillemot paste." But he had spent too much time yelling at her and now she had reached the shore. She climbed onto land. And when he tried to follow her there, everyone in the village came out and attacked him with their harpoons. Then they flensed him and removed every last bit of meat and blubber from his body.

All that remained of the whale were his bones, resting on the beach right next to the bones of an eagle.

Inugarssuk

THERE WAS AN old woman named Inugarssuk. She had been left behind on an island with her little granddaughter. Life wasn't so bad there except the granddaughter kept saying: "Grandma, tell me a story." And always Inugarssuk would answer: "I don't know any stories." Every time she lay down to sleep, the girl would say: "Tell me a story, tell me a story..."

Once the grandmother got so annoyed that she said: "Forget about stories. If you don't go to sleep, a horrible ghost will come and eat you. Look, you can see its face in the window now..."

Out of sheer fright the girl lost her human shape. She became smaller and smaller until she was small enough to slip through a crack in the wall. Inugarssuk rushed outside to look for her. She called the girl's name, but got no answer. Then she wandered about, crying, "Where is my grandchild? Where is my grandchild?" The rims of her eyes grew quite red from all this crying. Finally they grew so red that she turned into a ptarmigan. Her little granddaughter had become a sparrow. Sometimes they saw each other pecking for food in the snow.

The Giant Eider Duck

ONE MORNING A MAN named Kunuk woke up with a craving for eggs. So he paddled to an island and looked along the shore and soon located an eider duck's nest full of the largest eggs he'd ever seen. He gathered up these eggs and paddled back home. He was met by his wife who was crying and tearing at her hair.

"An enormous eider duck has come here and stolen our children!" she told him.

Kunuk leaped into his sledge and followed the tracks in the snow. He followed them all the way to the Inland Ice. At last he came to a cave in front of which was sitting an eider duck as large as the largest ice-bear.

"Since you have taken my children," the bird said, "I have decided to take yours..."

Kunuk threw his harpoon, but it only bounced off the eider duck's chest. Then he shot an arrow, and that also bounced off. In the end, he realized that he had to return the eggs or the eider duck would eat his children.

"As much as you people love your children," she told him, "we creatures love ours still more..."

The eider duck had turned and begun to walk away when Kunuk shot another arrow at her. This arrow hit a black spot at the back of her head, the only place where she could be killed. She dropped to the ground. And then Kunuk scooped up her eggs again and with his children climbed into the sledge.

"Eggs for supper, my dears," he said.

"How nice, daddy..."

They were nearly home when the sledge skidded on a rock and flipped over. Kunuk landed on the eggs and crushed them to pieces. The sledge itself landed on his children, and it likewise crushed them. Then the souls of the eider chicks and the souls of Kunuk's own children started out together on their journey to the Land of the Dead.

The She-Bear

ONCE THERE WERE TWO MEN named Papik and Ailaq. They were good friends who often shared each other's wives. But when they went hunting together, they did not share the same luck. It always seemed to happen that Ailaq would bring back a number of seals and Papik would come home with nothing but his jealousy. One day this Papik came home alone. Ailaq's mother asked him the whereabouts of her son.

"Oh, he fell into the sea."

Said the mother: "If he did, then you must have pushed him. You killed my son..."

"No, I didn't. He fell out of his kayak and drowned."

"...and I will avenge his death." Then she told Papik that she would eat him alive one day. At this he merely laughed and told her to go off and release her bowels in the snow rather than dump their contents on him.

The woman went down to the sea. She took along her bearskin rug and draped it over her entire body and let the incoming tide sweep her away.

A few years later a group of hunters were out on the floes. They saw a monstrous creature approaching them. It turned out to be a she-bear twice the size of a house, with burning coals for eyes and sharp knives for claws. The hunters started to run back toward the village. One of them was so terrified that he cut himself on his own harpoon. The others told him to run off in the opposite direction so that the bear would follow his trail of blood and not attack the village. Being an orphan boy, he did as he was told.

But the bear was too clever to be fooled by this tactic. It headed straight for the village. It went into Papik's house where Papik himself was cowering under his sleeping skins. In short order, the bear ripped his eyes, ears, and nose clean off his face. Then it dragged him twice through the village by his own intestines.

After eating what was left of Papik, the bear lay down to sleep. Cautiously the people approached it. But all they saw was the old woman's bearskin rug and a pile of bones covered with snails from the bottom of the sea.

The Wife Who Turned Into a Raven

IT WAS THE SAME old story: A man and wife were quarreling. She complained that he was no good as a husband. He complained that she would rather sleep with a certain young man named Pualuna than with him. Her tongue was sharper than a harpoonpoint. And he would stab at her legs with broken mussel shells. At last she could tolerate him no more. She went to an *angakok* and said: "Change me to some other creature, anything but a woman." He turned her into a raven. Now she could do as she pleased, fly where she wanted, and not worry about her husband. She made a nest in the mountains, and mated with another raven. But she found that she kept returning to her former home at night. As ravens cannot enter a human dwelling, she would sit outside and wait for a glimpse of her husband. "Oh, I wish he would come out and ease his bowels," she'd say to herself. She waited there night after night. Then one night he did come out to ease his bowels. She flew down, saying: "What lovely shit you have, my husband!" And at that moment she turned back into a woman. When her husband saw her, he took her for his wife again.

The Raven and The Hunter

A HUNTER FOUND AN excellent run of seal breathing holes. Then he searched around for a good place to camp. Along flew a raven,which pointed to a certain plain beneath a mountain. "There," the raven said, "all the hunters who come here camp there."

The man made his house where the raven indicated. But in the night a big boulder rolled down the mountain and crushed him to death.

"I don't know why all these hunters believe my silly stories," said the raven, pecking out the man's eyes.

"Am I Not a Handsome Brute?"

A MAN AND WOMAN had two very strong sons. They felt quite safe with these boys around the ice-hut. Nor did they ever suffer from want of food. Then one day the sons did not come home from a seal hunt. The father went out in search of them and found them hanging by their toes from a high cliff. This, he knew, was the work of Inlanders.

"Father! Help us!" the sons called down.

But the old man was not able to reach them. He kept climbing the cliffside and falling back down again.

"Help us! Help us!" the sons called, ever more feebly. And at last they died.

The parents went into mourning. They blackened their eyes with soot. They turned over their sledges and cried. They did not speak, eat, or venture out of their hut.

Five days later they were feeling somewhat better. But they knew they needed some sort of protection against the Inlanders. So they traded a pair of bearskin trousers for a whelp from a neighbor's dog. The woman nursed this dog on her own milk. By the end of winter, it had become a very large dog with an ability to speak just like a person. It would scratch its face, and say: "Am I not a handsome brute?"

"We have no ordinary dog on our hands," the old man said.

"Right," said the dog. "I am a charmed being."

One day the *angakok* foretold the arrival of Inlanders. They would come to the village and kill everybody. Whereupon the dog told its foster-parents that it was just going out for a little walk. It sniffed around and headed to where the Inlanders had made their camp. They were busy with the spirits of their dead. The dog

scratched itself, and said: "Am I not a handsome brute?" And the
Inlanders all fell to the ground, frightened to death.

The dog would catch seals in much the same way. Frighten
them out of the water. It was a better hunter than either of the
two dead sons.

Now the old couple began to fear this dog. They were afraid
that it would scratch itself around them. And then perhaps they
would die, too. So one day they instructed it to bring them home
some game. While it was away, they loaded their boat and set out
across the fjord. The dog came back, its mouth laded with ptarmigans. And when it saw its foster parents rowing away, it started to
howl. It followed them along the shore, howling and whining, until
they disappeared in the distance.

It is said that this is why dogs howl so much: they have a terrible
fear of being left alone by humans.

The Greedy Eagle

AN EAGLE SAW two rabbits running across the ice. He pounced on them, one under each foot. But they continued to run and now began dragging him along with them. The eagle's wife, who was watching all of this, said: "Let one of them loose." But he told her: "Winter is coming, and we'll soon be hungry. We need them both." "One is enough," she said. "One is never enough," he answered. Now the rabbits arrived at a big rock in the ice-field. One of them went to the left, the other to the right. The eagle kept his grasp on them, and he was torn in half. That evening rabbits came from far and wide to dine on eagle.

The Eider Duck's Revenge

ONCE SOME PEOPLE were playing a game of ball. Suddenly an eider duck flew overhead. The ball struck the bird and brought it to the ground. The people thought this quite amusing and rushed over to the eider duck before it could get up. In great merriment, they plucked off all its feathers. Now it was nothing but a bare naked creature. The people thought this quite amusing, too.

At last the bird was able to fly away. It flew to a rock and just stood there shivering, for it could not protect itself against the cold. Yet even as it was shivering, it began to brew up a terrible rage in its chest. "They will be sorry," it said to itself, "that they treated me so miserably."

Now winter came, and the snows were deep and the cold worse than any cold in many years. As a result, quite a few people starved to death. The rest kept to their ice-huts and survived only by eating clothes and the corpses of their kin. That year summer arrived as late as anyone could remember.

Such was the result of the eider duck's rage in its chest.

Guillemots

MANY YEARS AGO a group of children were playing next to a large ravine. Their noise seemed to disturb an old man who was sitting by a seal's breathing-hole. The man thought: If there are any seals left in the sea, they will never pick this breathing-hole. Finally he shouted to the children: "May the walls of that rock close on you, little good-for-nothings!"

And that is precisely what happened. The children were buried in rock. Their parents came along and tried to hammer an opening for them, but it was no use. Then the parents saw the old man, his ear to the breathing-hole. "I was the one who put them there," he told them.

"Why did you do such a thing to our children?"

"Because they were a damned nuisance," he shrugged.

"Well, in that case, may you be turned to ice forever!"

And that is precisely what happened. The man's wife found him, a statue of ice, sitting by the breathing-hole. She tried to scrape away some of the ice, but the more she scraped, the smaller the man became. In the end, she scraped all of him away. Now there was nothing for her to do but go back home and search around for a new husband.

Meanwhile, the parents kept returning to their children, as they hoped to find some way to release them from the rock. They could even hear the children crying inside—in particular, one little girl who had a baby with her and who kept telling it, "Don't worry, little one. Mother will be here soon..." The mother heard this and called upon the local *angakok* to help her poor children. The *angakok* went on a spirit flight and was gone for several days. "I think I have the answer," he said upon his return. Then he beat his drum and chanted loudly and passed his hands again and again over the rock. All at once the children turned into guillemots and flew up out of the crevices. They flew over the sea, and away. At last they were free.

The Lustful Raven

ONCE THERE WAS A raven whose wife was killed by humans. Being very lustful, he needed a new wife right away. He happened upon a little sparrow whose husband had been killed by humans, too.

"Oh, my husband was so sweet," the sparrow said, "for he used to catch nice fat worms for me."

Replied the raven: "I'll be your husband now. We'll make love all night long. I'll give you lovely shit to eat."

"Unfortunately," said the sparrow, "that doesn't appeal to me."

So the raven flew away—again to seek a new wife. Soon he met a ptarmigan whose husband had left her.

"Yes," said the ptarmigan, "he left me because he wanted to exchange wives and I did not feel like sleeping with a fulmar."

The raven asked her to be his wife.

"I could never do that," she said. "You have such a high forehead and your beak is much too big for your face. You're really quite ugly, you know."

So the raven continued his search for a new wife. By now he was so lustful that he was unable to sleep. At last he came to a flock of wild geese, two of whom he picked out, saying: "Since that damned ptarmigan turned me down, I'm twice as lustful as before. I think I'll take the two of you to wife."

"But we're just getting ready to leave this place," the geese told him.

The raven said that he'd go with them.

"But you can neither swim or rest on the water," they said.

"I'll manage ..."

Whereupon the raven flew away with the geese. They flew for

some distance over open water. Now the raven was getting rather tired. "Lie down on the sea, you two," he said to his wives.

The wives did as they were told. Soon the raven was making love to them, first the one, then the other. In the middle of his love-making, however, the wives saw their comrades flying farther and farther away. And they rose up to join them. The raven fell into the water, gasping:

"Come back here, you two! Come back and get together! I need something to sit on..."

But they had already flown away. The raven sank to the bottom of the sea where he was transformed into thousands of tiny black snails, each calling to the other: "Get together, get together..."

Tiggak

THERE WAS A MAN named Tiggak whose only son drowned in the sea. And such a powerful grief came to the old man that he set up his hut right next to this son's grave. The very first night he was awakened by noises. An ice-bear, a walrus, a hare, and a fox were busy removing the stones from the grave. Tiggak was furious and threatened them with his spear.

"But how do you think that we get our teeth?" said the fox.

"How do you think that we got our whiskers?" the walrus said.

"And how do you think we got our genitals?" the hare said.

"We must perforce steal from the dead," declared the ice bear.

Whereupon Tiggak allowed them to take whatever they wanted from his son. The grateful animals repaid his kindness many times over, for there wasn't a day after that when he didn't have good hunting.

VI. Death & Old Age

The Collector of Ravens

THERE WAS A young boy whose mother was making him some raven-skin trousers. She needed just one more raven to complete these trousers. So the boy went outside and searched around until he saw a raven, which he killed. Just then an old man came along with a pile of dead ravens on his back.

"That's my raven," said the old man. "Kindly give it to me."

"Oh no," replied the boy. "It's mine, and I need it for my trousers."

"If you don't give it to me, you'll be in trouble..."

The boy simply laughed and proceeded to skin the bird.

Said the old man: "You are doomed."

Now the boy began walking home with the raven-skin. All at once he felt quite weary. His legs crumpled under him and he could no longer walk, only crawl. He crawled on his hands and knees until he reached his mother's hut. "Let me in! Mother, let me in!"

His mother came out of the hall-passage. "Who are you?" she said.

"I am your son."

"No, you're not. You're a tired old man and I've never seen you before."

But she took pity on him and brought him inside. Then he began to tell her the story of what happened when he killed the raven. As he talked, his hair turned white and his face became wrinkled. At the moment he finished telling the story, the boy died of old age.

Meqqoq and the Stone People

AN OLD WOMAN named Meqqoq was just minding her own business when she was grabbed by two large stones disguised as human beings. They were husband and wife, and they took Meqqoq back home as their child. Now they removed her clothes and began to fondle her, saying: "How smooth your skin is, little daughter! How nice and smooth!"

They carried her around in an *amaut* sack just as though she were a baby. They chewed food for her and wiped her. And always they fondled her, saying: "Such a dear little daughter we have!"

Again and again she would tell them that she was an old woman. But it did no good. They would simply give her dolls and string figures to play with. And, of course, fondle her until her skin seemed ready to fall off.

After a few weeks in this place, Meqqoq's loins turned to stone. She was fearful that the rest of her would turn to stone as well, so she asked her parents if she could have her clothing back.

The stone woman replied: "You would only run away and that would break our hearts."

"I am just so cold," Meqqoq said.

The stone man told her: "Do we not fondle you enough? Do we not make your flesh warm? Here, eat your reindeer tallow."

One day Meqqoq located her clothing under a pile of small rocks that was her parents' shit-heap. She waited until they were off hunting reindeer and then she made her escape. All night she could hear avalanches crashing down the mountains, and her parents calling: "Little daughter!! Little daughter! Please come back, little daughter!"

But she paid no heed to them. After several days of walking, she came at last to her own home. Now she settled back to her old life, chewing leather and such-like. However, her loins remained stone for the rest of her days.

The Magic Bear

ONCE THERE LIVED an old couple who did not have any children. The woman was thin and wrinkled, yet this couple still hoped to have a child somehow. One day, after he had killed an ice-bear, the old man took some of the blood and passed his hands over it, singing:

"Blood be flesh
flesh be fur
dear bear, dear bear
come alive to me..."

At which point the blood turned into a little bear. The old couple fondled it, fed it, and took it into their sleeping skins with them. At length it was able to hunt harbor seals for its house-parents. Then it went after ringed seals. Once it even brought back a walrus. At last there came a day when the old man asked it to bring back an ice-bear. He said he liked nothing better than a big fresh slab of ice-bear meat. The bear was very upset by this, for it did not want to hunt a fellow creature. But the old man insisted, saying: "I am the house-father here. And you must do as I say."

And so the bear went off and brought back a big she-bear, which the old couple cut up into steaks. They ate these steaks that same night. After dinner, the bear left the house and did not return in the morning. Nor did it return the next morning. Both man and woman sang:

"Flesh of our flesh
blood of our blood
dear bear, dear bear
come back home to us..."

But the bear did not come back. The old people sang and wept and, in a short while, died.

The Kayaker Who Flew

THERE WAS AN old bachelor who could not tolerate singing of any sort. If there was a drum dance in his village, he would hasten away on a dead run. If a pretty young woman was singing, he would tell her to shut up. One day, however, he heard singing that he liked. It came from the crew of a boat which was moving against the wind. Several times this boat seemed to dance in the air above the fjord. Nobody seemed to be rowing it. The old bachelor paddled his kayak toward the boat so that he could hear the words more clearly: "Let us fly through the air, *ah, ha, aja…*" "Lovely," he said. "You want to join us?" the men asked him. And when he said yes, they tied his kayak to their boat and all together they began to rise into the sky. He did not need to paddle anymore. Now he sang as loudly and lustily as the others. They flew over mountain after mountain until they landed on a very high peak. Here lived the men with their wives, who were eagles. The bachelor was made to feel very much at home. One of the men lent him his wife for the night. They loaded his kayak with seal meat and fat, and the eagles loaded it with rabbits. "Henceforth," they told him, "you must continue your journey without us." He climbed into his kayak and started to sing and lo! he was flying through the air all by himself. He flew around for days. He could see the whole world beneath him. What a clever fellow am I, he thought. Nobody else from my village can do this. And he decided to fly home and show off his airborne powers. As he was turning around his kayak, he forgot the words to the song. "*Imakaja, ha, ha…*" No, that wasn't it. "*Mamaq, ikaja…*" Not that, either. Now his kayak was plummeting down to earth. He flailed about with his arms. He threw the seal meat and rabbits overboard, but he

continued to fall. At the last moment, however, he remembered
the words. And his kayak rose up and he directed it home. He did
not stop until he crashed through the door to his own little hut,
kayak and all. After that the old bachelor did not take to the air
nor did he ever sing again.

The Old Woman Who
Was Kind to Insects

ONE WINTER THERE WAS an old woman who was left behind.
She was so old that she couldn't even chew *kamik* leather anymore. Her family left her with only a few insects to eat. The
woman said: "I'm not going to eat these poor creatures. I am old
and perhaps they are young. Perhaps even a few are children. I'd
rather die first..."

Just after her people went away, there entered a fox into her
hut. It leaped up and started to bite her. The old woman thought:
Well, I'm truly a dead person now... But the fox was behaving in
a very strange manner. It was biting her over her whole body, just
like it was taking off her clothing. Soon all her skin fell away. And
lo! there was a new skin beneath which belonged to an attractive
young woman. For the grateful insects had instructed their friend
the fox to rid her of her old skin.

Next summer her family returned to the camp. But they found
neither the woman or her bones. She had gone to live with the
insects. It is said that she married a little blow-fly of whom she
had grown quite fond.

Natatoq, the Storyteller

THIS NATATOQ WAS A very ancient fellow who had outlived
his wife and all his children. His wife had died of the burning
sickness. Some of his children had died of hunger, others from
avalanches and such-like. His eldest son had been snatched by
some nasty folk with iron tails who dwelled on the island of
Norssit. The Norssit folk killed the boy and cut off his sexual
organs and bound them round his head so that they hung down
over his eyes. Of all the deaths of his children, this death grieved
the old man the most.

Near Natatoq's hut was a longhouse where lived a family of
seven brothers. Often the old man would be invited to this longhouse because he could tell stories to shorten the winter. He
would tell of the old *angakoks* who combed Nerrivik's hair. He
would talk of a time when there were as many musk-oxen and
reindeer as *nunataks* in the Inland Ice. Yet it seemed that the
brothers were more eager to hear about the deaths of Natatoq's
children. Always they would ask the old man to recount how each
of his children had died. Likewise they wanted him to describe his
own sorrow. Just how terrible is it, old man, to lose your entire
family? Were you not sad when your little girl fell into the sea?
And always Natatoq would have to describe these deaths in pain-
ful detail. For he was too old to hunt and the only way he obtained
meat was from the brothers.

Now Natatoq had long kept secret the story of his eldest son.
He figured that he would die himself if he had to tell it. But
somehow the brothers found out and they asked him about this
son's death. They asked him to repeat the boy's name again and
again. And when he finished and told of how he felt when he saw

his son's penis in the middle of his face, the brothers collapsed in laughter. Then they tossed him a piece of backbone with a little meat clinging to it.

Afterwards the old man hurried home and threw himself to the floor, sobbing. He lay on the floor for quite some time. At last he began to rage against the brothers. He peered through the holes of the backbone, saying:

"Come alive, little friend, and avenge my sorrow."

He threw the backbone outside his hut where it became an enormous skeleton, tall as ten men, walking toward the brothers' longhouse. It sat down outside their door. They were so frightened that they could not move. They could not eat, drink, or even blink their eyes. They simply remained seated, facing the skeleton. And as this happened, Natatoq felt himself getting younger and younger. He thought: I will settle in a place which does not have so many bad memories. Whereupon he got in his old kayak and paddled away.

It wasn't long before he came to a flat, grassy promontory. There he hunted for a year. But, young and robust now, he craved a woman. And so he set out in search of one. As he was walking in the mountains one day, he was joined by an Inland Dweller, who told him: "Why don't you come back with me to my village? We have many more women than men. They would be most eager to lie with you."

Natatoq followed him to his village. It was built on a thin strip of land where the Inland Ice met the sea. Inland Dwellers greeted him and held a drum-dance and feast in his honor. A man offered him one of his wives. She was very pretty, but had rather unpleasant eyes. And that night Natatoq's worst suspicions about her were fulfilled: After they had lain together, the girl made an attempt to rip off his testicles. He grabbed her, however, and squeezed her so hard that she could not breathe. When her husband came to lie with her, he discovered that he was lying with a dead person. He called out to the village: "Natatoq has killed my dear little wife. We must find him and, at the very least, cut off his head."

All the Inland Dwellers now began to chase Natatoq, chanting: Kill! Kill! Kill!

Meanwhile the skeleton that held the brothers under an enchantment was crumbling away. The more it crumbled, the more they stirred into life. At last it was little more than a few specks of dust on the ground. The brothers bolted out the door, determined to find Natatoq and make him pay for what he had done to them. They climbed into their kayaks and paddled out of the fjord.

From one direction the Inland Dwellers were after him. Natatoq hastened over mountains and fled toward the sea where he saw the brothers paddling furiously toward him. Now he turned around. The Inland Dwellers were gaining on him. He ran behind a big boulder that stood alone by the sea. The brothers and the Inland Dwellers converged on the boulder at the same time, each demanding the right to kill him. But when they looked behind, they found nothing—only clothes, kamiks, and a flensing knife. Natatoq was not there. He had entered the Great Solitude.

The Hole in the Cliffs

A LITTLE BOY lived with his grandfather. The grandfather stuck
to his sleeping skins, for he was old and feeble. One day he said to
the boy: "Never visit such-and-such a place in the cliffs. There is
an enormous hole there. You might fall in."

"And what will happen if I do fall in?" asked the boy.

Replied the grandfather: "You will end up in the Land of the
Dead."

This made the boy very curious about the hole. He climbed up
to it that very same day. As he approached it, he smelled a horrible odor. He could not imagine a worse odor in all the world.
Then he came to the hole itself. It seemed to be alive, getting
bigger and smaller and then bigger again.

The boy started throwing stones into the hole. He nearly died
from the smell. At last he succeeded in filling the hole completely
with stones. Then he went home, only to discover his grandfather
dead on the floor. For the hole in the cliffs was the old man's ass
hole and the boy had killed him by blocking it up.

The Old Man Who Ate His Grandson

THERE WAS AN old man who was left at home to mind his grandson. The boy was a strong, healthy little fellow. The old man gazed at him for quite a long time. A deep hunger gnawed in his stomach. Suddenly he tossed the boy into the stewpot, cooked him, and ate him. When the mother came back, she found that she no longer had a son. But she did not make mention of the matter to the old man. No one in the village mentioned it to him. One year passed, two years, and still no one mentioned it to him. Then one day he went with the others to hunt seals. It was a bitter cold day, the wind blowing, ice in the hair. The men caught their first seal and the liver was passed around. As the old man was cutting off his piece of the liver, the others grabbed him and pressed him to the ground. His son-in-law came over and stripped him of all his clothing. Now the old man would freeze to death if he did not get back to the village. And somehow he did manage to walk back despite the wind and snow against his skin. But when he bent over to enter his house, his backbone cracked. Then his body broke into several frozen pieces. And so it was that the old man arrived in the Land of the Dead not as a human being but as pieces of ice.

Umaq, Who Danced

A MAN NAMED Umaq who used to say that he would dance after his death. Every time he said this, people would laugh at him. They would tell him that they were quite eager for him to die because they had never seen a corpse dance. Or they would ask him why he wanted to dance in death when he never danced in life.

At length the old man died. Several days later there was a party during which Umaq's promise was remembered. Some men thought it would be great fun to ask the dead man to dance. So they piled into a boat and rowed over to the grave mound where he was buried. Someone called out: "Hey, Old Man Umaq! How about a dance performance for us?"

And at that moment Umaq appeared, sitting on his grave. His naked body was all yellow and withered, already starting to decay. He stood up and removed a long bone from his left arm. Then he began to dance, beating his pelvis with this bone. He sang: "Mother Ocean, Mother Ocean, come to me..."

An enormous wave rose up from the sea and moved towards Umaq. It struck the boat so violently that it nearly turned over. Now the men grew rather frightened. They pleaded with Umaq to stop dancing. But the more they pleaded, the harder he danced, singing: "Mother Ocean, Mother Ocean, come to me..."

Again an enormous wave struck the boat. And again the men yelled, "Stop dancing, Umaq! Please, please stop dancing!" But the dead man only grinned, and danced on, calling to Mother Ocean. The boat rocked wildly back and forth. At last a wave came which reached up nearly to the clouds. This wave buried the boat, men and all, with icy seawater. Everyone drowned. Umaq danced on, and slowly returned to the earth.

Never mock a dead man.

Tuglik and Her Granddaughter

ONCE THERE WAS A big narwhal hunt to which everyone went but an old woman named Tuglik and her granddaughter Qujapik. The two of them were getting rather hungry, but they hadn't any idea of how to hunt for their food. Yet old Tuglik knew a few magical words, which she uttered during a trance. All of a sudden she changed into a man. She had a seal-bone for a penis and a chunk of *mataq* for testicles. Her vagina became a sledge. She said to her granddaughter:

"Now I can travel to the fjords and get some food for us."

The girl replied: "But what about dogs to pull your sledge?"

And so strong was the old woman's magic that she was able to create a team of dogs from her own lice. The dogs were barking and yelping and ready to go, so Tuglik cracked her whip and off she went with them to the fjords. Day after day she went off like this, and she would always return in the evening with some sort of game, even if it was only a ptarmigan or two. Once, while she was away hunting, a man came to their hut. He looked around and said:

"Whose harpoon is this, little girl?"

"Oh," said Qujapik, "it is only my grandmother's."

"And whose kayak is this?"

"Just my grandmother's."

"You seem to be pregnant. Who is your husband?"

"My grandmother is my husband."

"Well, I know someone who would make a better husband for you..."

Now the old woman returned home with a walrus thrown over her sledge. "Qujapik" she called out. "Qujapik!" But there

Qujapik at all. The girl had gathered up all her things and left the village with her new husband.

Tuglik saw no point in being a man anymore—man or woman, it's all the same when a person is alone. So she uttered her magic words and once again she was a wrinkled old hag with a vagina instead of a sledge.

Old Age

THERE WAS A woman who was old, blind, and likewise unable to walk. Once she asked her daughter for a drink of water. The daughter was so bored with her old mother that she gave her a bowl of her own piss. The old woman drank it all up, then said: "You're a nice one, daughter. Tell me—which would you prefer as a lover, a louse or a sea scorpion?"

"Oh, a sea scorpion," laughed the daughter, "because he would not be crushed so easily when I slept with him."

Whereupon the old woman proceeded to pull sea scorpions out of her vagina, one after another, until she fell over dead.

The Old Seal-Hunter From Aluk

THERE WAS AN old seal-hunter from Aluk and he loved his native place so much that he never had the notion to leave it. Nor had he ever left it in all his long years of life. One by one everyone in the village went away, and few of them ever seemed to come back. Not this fellow. He said he would die if he could not see the sun rising up as it always rose up in Aluk.

The old man's son wanted to pick up and move on to some better place. There were fewer seals in Aluk than ever before. Winters were worse. There were no women. And so on. The boy said to his father: "The world is big. Don't you think it's time that we should journey out and take a look at it?"

To which the father replied: "Why look at the world when we can look at Aluk? Why travel when we can stay put?"

"Well, I'm afraid that I'll have to go without you," said the son.

The old man did not want to be left behind, so he joined his son. Next day they paddled out of Aluk. They went south along the coast, toward Cape Farewell. And though the weather was fine and the seals plentiful, the old man began to wish that he was home. Indeed, the more the summer advanced, the more powerful his native place appeared in his memory. He would get up early in the morning to watch for the sunrise. But it always seemed to be blocked by mountains. Or there was always too much rain or fog. Finally he spoke to his son about it. He said he would die if he could not see the sun rise up in the heavens as it rose up in Aluk.

"But don't you think that this is a beautiful country, too?" the boy asked him.

"It has too many mountains and they are forever blocking off the sun . . ."

"But aren't they beautiful mountains?"

"I prefer the little rocks of home..."

Now the old seal-hunter became sick and his son decided that they had better go back home. They packed their goods and paddled until they reached Aluk. Then the old man went to sleep. Next morning he got up early in order to see the sunrise.

Ah, thought his son, he is better already. For he could hear his father shouting with joy outside. But all at once the old man was silent. The boy ran out and saw his father lying dead on the ground, his face turned in the direction of the sun.

For the old man had once again seen the sun rise at Aluk and his delight was so great that it burst his heart.

"I Have Sent Them My Death..."

ONCE UPON A TIME there was an old woman and she was so feeble that she could hardly get up from her sleeping platform. She had to rely on hand-outs from her neighbors. Yet people were not too happy about giving her their food. "What's the use?" they asked. "She's old, she'll die soon, and then we won't have enough food to last us through the winter."

At length the old woman grew quite weary of the meanness of her neighbors. All that remained of her now was her skeleton. She bent over and placed her skull against her vagina and sang a charm song. The skull grew to such an enormous size that it broke off from the rest of her body. Whereupon it proceeded to roll around the village. Many people were frightened to death when they saw the skull, and many others ran away and never returned to their homes. However, the old woman's little grandson recognized the skull and he asked what was wrong. What was the point of frightening everyone to death? She replied:

"I have sent them my death so that they would see the consequences of not feeding a fellow human being..."

Then she picked up her skull and stuck it back on her neck and threw herself into the sea.

The Man and His Wife
Who Raised the Dead

ONCE THERE WAS A man and woman whose only son fell off a cliff and died. Now the couple had nobody to provide for them, as the man himself was too feeble to venture out in a kayak. They wondered how they would obtain food. At last the old man said: "I know. Let's dig up a grave..."

"But I'm not very fond of corpse meat," his wife protested.

"Well," he told her, "there are a great many things you can do with a corpse besides eat it..."

So they went out and the woman, as was her job, dug up a grave. This grave belonged to a young hunter drowned at sea. His corpse was greatly decayed. But the old man began to chant some magic words and the decay fell away, revealing a very healthy body underneath. The old man continued to chant and first the young hunter sat up, then he stood up. He tried to strangle the old woman, but the magic words overcame him. Whereupon he gazed warmly at her and said: "Mother..."

"You must provide for us," the old man told him, "because we can't provide for ourselves."

"That I will gladly do, father."

And the young man brought them whatever they wanted. In many ways, he was a better son than their first son.

Then it happened that the boy's real father showed up. He saw that the top-stone on the grave had been moved and he accused the old couple of digging up his son's dead body and eating it. The old man told him to wait till dusk, when the boy would return from hunting. Then he would see if his son had been eaten. The father agreed to do this. He waited and at last the boy appeared with a big Greenland seal. The father rushed up to him.

"No!" exclaimed the old man. "Don't do that!"

But it was too late. The father hugged his son, who immediately decayed back to his former condition.

"You can't touch him," said the old man. "You can talk with him, but you can't touch him." Then he chanted the magic words again. And once again the boy became a living person. When he saw his father, he tried to strangle him, saying: "You left me before the five mourning days were over..."

The old man chanted on and the boy took his hands from his father's neck. However, he was still upset about being left before the five mourning days were over. At last the father had to go away because the son would not acknowledge him. And once again the boy became the old couple's son.

Time passed. One day the boy came back and announced that he had fallen in love with a girl who was the daughter of Inland Dwellers. She had a face a little like a dog's, but that was all right. He wanted to take her to wife. Who will look after us now? the old man asked him. And he replied:

"You can come with me, dear parents. My new wife and I will look after you."

He strapped the two old people to his kayak and paddled away with them. He paddled to a place which neither the man or the woman had ever seen before. The ice-mountains were of a very strange formation, and the rivers seemed to flow away from the sea rather than toward it. There was a beach on which stood huge piles of flesh, blubber, and *mataq*. The old man and woman had never seen so much food in all their lives.

The boy said: "Here is the beginning of the Inland Dwellers' land. Now you must promise me one thing. Never touch any of this meat. Let me feed you, or my wife feed you. It will go very bad for us if you don't..."

Then they landed on the beach. In his joy, the old man forgot all about not touching the meat. He reached out to grab a nice piece of seal liver. Suddenly everything disappeared, and the boy again started to decay. The old man tried his magic words, but they did not work now. In a very short while, the boy was little more than a moldering heap of bones.

"Oh, my son, my poor son!" cried the old woman, wringing her hands.

They buried the bones. And once again they were merely a lonely old couple with no one in the world to feed them.

Skeletons

THERE WAS A FAMILY of skeletons in a little hut. They had starved to death, but they still survived—a grandfather skeleton, an uncle skeleton, a father skeleton, a mother skeleton, two little boy skeletons, and a baby skeleton. They managed quite well because they never needed anything to eat. But one day a hunter came and stayed in their hut. The skeletons emerged from the ground and began to sing and beat their drums. The hunter burst into laughter. "You are only skeletons," he said. "Stop behaving as if you were human beings." And the skeletons were so ashamed that they retreated to the ground and never beat their drums again.

Kivioq, Whose Kayak Was Full of Ghosts

THERE WAS A MAN named Kivioq whose wife died. He had been very fond of her. He buried her under a pile of stones and then lay down to sleep away her death. But he was unable to rid himself of her. He woke up even sadder than before. So he decided to leave the place where he lived and travel away far away from his memories.

All at once his little son, whom he planned to leave behind, burst through the door. The boy had a big smile on his face and he said: "I've just seen mother. She's outside with another man."

"Your mother is dead," Kivioq said. But he went outside to look for himself anyway. And, sure enough, there was his wife rubbing stomachs with a man whom he did not know. Neither paid any attention to him.

Kivioq was furious. He struck down both his wife and the other man and buried them in a second grave. "Now," he said to his wife, "perhaps you will stay dead." And then he made good resolve to flee from that place. While his little boy slept, he packed his goods into his kayak and hastened away. He was already quite a distance across the fjord when he thought he heard the boy calling for him to come back. But he paddled on.

Now Kivioq was attacked by sea-lice. They ate up half the skin from his kayak. Then he was nearly sucked into a whirlpool. As he paddled out of the whirlpool, a Claw-Troll scratched at his eyes. Then he came upon two icebergs. He was unable to paddle around them. Well, he thought, I'll just paddle between them. And as he went between them, suddenly the icebergs closed on him and he was almost crushed to death. It was with some relief that he turned his kayak toward land.

But his troubles were only beginning. Once he pulled onto the shore, he met a woman who gestured for him to enter her house. He followed her inside. There he saw another woman—a wrinkled old creature whose dugs reached almost to her toes—lying on some tattered sleeping skins. This old woman offered him berries mixed with fat, which he ate with great gusto. "These taste very fine," he said as he chewed.

"Small wonder," replied the old woman, "for the fat is from a very young man."

Now Kivioq feigned sleep. And he heard the two women talking away: "Let's kill him now," the old one said. "I'm hungry."

"No," said the young one. "Let's wait. I want the chance to make love with him first."

"Well, let me have the first taste of his head, then. It's been a long time since I tasted head."

"All right, but I want his genitals. Especially if he turns out to be a good lover..."

Whereupon Kivioq jumped up and dashed out the door. After a while he came to another house inside which lived only a baby. This baby had an enormous, bloated stomach. All around were various frozen parts of bodies. The baby took one look at Kivioq and said: "How nice of mother and grandmother to send me over some fresh food..."

If the sea is dangerous, Kivioq thought, then the land is twice as bad. He ran back to his kayak. He had hardly set out when an eagle swept down and tried to carry him off. He escaped only by smashing the eagle's head with his paddle. Then the ghosts of drowned people rose up from the water and sat on his kayak, for they hoped to drown him as they themselves had been drowned. Yet Kivioq paddled on, despite so much extra weight.

Now he was joined by the ghosts of his wife and her lover. The drowned people complained that there wasn't enough room for all of them on the kayak. But the wife and her lover found a place anyway. She said to Kivioq:

"It was very unkind of you to kill me."

"But you were already dead..."

"To kill a person who is already dead," she said, "that is the unkindest thing of all..."

Years seemed to pass with all these ghosts on the back of his kayak. He seemed to paddle everywhere, up and down every fjord, everywhere in the entire country. Each year the kayak got heavier and heavier, but he paddled on. At last he came upon a number of other kayaks and they were dragging along a huge whale. On the back of this whale stood a very robust young man. Kivioq recognized this young man as his own son. He hailed him: "I am your father, dear boy. I am old Kivioq."

But his son did not recognize him. "Oh, that could not be true. My father died years ago. He was sucked down into a whirlpool. You're just a crazy old man in a kayak full of ghosts." Then the son was pulled away by the others.

And old Kivioq buried his head in his arms and wept.

What is the Earth?

THREE FRIENDS WERE curious about the size and shape of the earth. They were so curious that they decided to go exploring. They had traveled for three days and two nights when they came to an enormous ice-house. "Let's go in," one of the friends said. And so they went into the house, which seemed to be without end. They followed the walls in order not to get lost. Where was the passage through which they'd entered? They walked for days, for months, for years. At last they grew very weary. It was all they could do to crawl now. Then two of the friends could no longer crawl and they sat down and died. The third friend managed to find the exit-passage. His kayak was exactly where he'd left it. He came back to his people as a very old man. And he told them: "The earth is simply a very big ice-house."

Then he died too.

GLOSSARY

akutaq—an ice cream-like desert

amaut—the hooded pouch in which a woman carries her child

angakok—shaman or witch doctor; more recently, a healer

kamik—sealskin or bearskin boot; perhaps the most important item of apparel in the North

kapataq—hooded foxskin jacket

kiviaq—a dish of putrified guillemots; a delicacy in Northern Greenland

mataq—whale skin

nunatak—a mountain sticking out of the Greenland Ice Cap

qivigtoq—in folklore, a sort of holy hermit; in reality, an insane person who has been banished to the mountains

seqijuk—a worthless individual

toornaq—an *angakok's* helping spirit

Tuneq, pl. *Tunit*—an imaginary people who sometimes make their homes in the depths of the earth and sometimes on the Greenland Ice Cap

tupilak—an evil spirit or sending; a *tupilak* can be made to resemble any living creature

ulu—a woman's knife

umiaq—a large boat, usually rowed by women

Sources of the Tales

I. ORIGINS AND ANCESTORS

The Woman of the Sea. Versions heard in Greenland, Labrador, and throughout the Arctic

Sun and Moon. Throughout the Arctic.

The Origin of Daylight. Told by Jeremiah Obed, Nain, Labrador.

The Louse and the Worm. Heard from Robert Petersen, folklorist, Nuuq, West Greenland.

The Birth of Fog. Collected from a man named Nattiq during a seal hunt. Near Gjoa Haven, Northwest Territories.

The Thunder Children. Heard throughout the Arctic and Greenland.

The Girl Who Married Her Dog. From the Arctic and Greenland.

Sila, the Weather Spirit. Narrated by Ken Annanack, schoolteacher and plumber, on a hike through Auyuittuq National Park, Baffin Island.

The Origin of Women. Man in bar, Frobisher Bay, Baffin Island, who heard the story in Aklavik, Northwest Territories.

The Origin of Wind. Heard on a windy day. Outdoor market. Nuuq, West Greenland.

The Pleiades. Akpaleeapik ("Little Murre"), Pond Inlet, Baffin Island.

The First Narwhal. Told by Ken Annanack, Pangnirtung ("Place of the Bull Caribou"), Baffin Island, to his daughter.

The Father of Fish. Throughout the Arctic and Greenland.

Mosquitoes. Overheard in Narsarssuaq, mosquito capital of the world. West Greenland.

The Origin of Sharks. Angmagssalik, East Greenland.

The First Walrus. Collected from Elijah Saimat, from Nain, Labrador, who was undergoing treatment for pneumonia at the Grenfell Hospital in St. Anthony, Newfoundland.

Flies. Heard at the Navigator Inn, Frobisher Bay, Baffin Island.

Of Giants And Human Beings. Told by an airline stewardess in the Fort Chimo airport, Quebec.

Killing People Is Wrong. From Jørgen Skansen, sixty-year-old fisherman, Saqqaq, West Greenland.

II. CHILDREN

Kakuarshuk. Collected from Severin Lynge, Rittenbeck, West Greenland.

The Northern Lights Children. Heard throughout the Arctic and Greenland.

The Child Who Lived In All Things. Narrated by Anarfiik ("Sweet Piss-Hole"), Sermiligaq, East Greenland.

The Unwanted Child. Cashier, Royal Greenland Trading Post, Angmagssalik, East Greenland.

The Boy Who Was Raised By Foxes. Old man untangling his dog traces. Near Cape Dorset, Baffin Island.

Ussarqak, Who Ate Too Many Heads. Told by Nattiq during a banquet of Arctic char and raw seal heart. Near Gjoa Haven, Northwest Territories.

Qituarssuk. Collected in Labrador and West Greenland.

Arviaq and the Worm. Told by Ib Brodersen, seal hunter, Angmagssalik, East Greenland.

Qalaganguase, Who Had No Strength. From George Inukpasugjuk. At his summer camp during the netting of whitefish. Near Gjoa Haven, Northwest Territories.

The Spoon Monster. Pond Inlet, Baffin Island.

Tulugaq, Who Was Barren. From Anarfiik's wife, Meqqoq ("Hairy Woman"). Sermiligaq, East Greenland.

The Monstrous Child. Collected from Ib Brodersen, Angmagssalik, East Greenland.

Anarteq. Told by Ken Annanack, Pangnirtung, Baffin Island.

204

III. MAGIC AND TABOOS

"The Earth Will Know." Eskimo Point, Northwest Territories.

Every Taboo Is Holy. Old woman, drunk. Cape Dorset, Baffin Island.

The Sick Raven. Versions heard in Northwest Territories and East Greenland.

The House of Reindeer. Heard from Severin Lynge, Rittenbeck, West Greenland, in the midst of cutting up a reindeer.

The Cure. Taxi driver. Frobisher Bay, Baffin Island.

Katerparsuk, the Orphan. From Gustav Broberg, seal hunter, Kulusuk, East Greenland.

Bad Food. Schoolteacher, Godhavn, West Greenland.

The Rival Angakoks. Collected from Anarfiik on an icy summer day, Sermiligaq, East Greenland.

The Spirit of the Shitpile. From George Inukpasugjuk at his whitefish camp. Near Gjoa Haven, Northwest Territories.

The Entrail Thief. Throughout West Greenland.

Him-Whose-Penis-Stretches-Down-To-His-Knees. Man in International Harvester Cap and Nike sneakers. Kulusuk, East Greenland.

"I Am Only Shit". Heard throughout the Arctic.

The Brother-in-law Who Became a Bear. Collected from Ken Annanack in the Auyuittuq National Park, Baffin Island.

A Tale of Motherlove. Jeremiah Obed, Nain, Labrador.

The Feasting House Ghost. Pond Inlet, Baffin Island.

Don't Forget to Pray. Cashier, Royal Greenland Trading Post, Angmagssalik, East Greenland.

Niarqoq. Man carving a *tupilak*. Kulusuk, East Greenland.

Namik. Fort Chimo, Quebec.

The Lame Man's Stick. Heard during a *kaffemik* ("coffee orgy"). Jakobshavn, West Greenland.

Erdlaversissoq. Versions heard throughout the Arctic and Greenland.

IV. HUMAN BEINGS

The Glutton. Collected in Saqqaq, West Greenland.

Imarasugssuaq. Kulusuk, East Greenland.

The Fox-Wife and the Penis of the Lake. Narrated by Ib Brodersen, flensing a seal. Angmagssalik, East Greenland.

Blubber Boy. Collected throughout the Arctic and Greenland.

Uutaaq, the Hunter. Told as a joke at a birthday party. Eskimo Point, Northwest Territories.

Counting Hairs. Told by Ken Annanack, Pangnirtung, Baffin Island, at the anniversary party for the big wind which took away his home, the local nursing station, the community garage, and half the Hudson Bay Store.

Utsuuq. Collected from Gustav Broberg. Kulusuk, East Greenland.

The Sisters Who Married Erqigdlit. Jørgen Skansen, Saqqaq, West Greenland.

The Ghost That Ate Children. Collected from Anarfiik during an all-night chat about the behavior of ghosts. Sermiligaq, East Greenland.

Evat. Fort Chimo, Quebec.

The Two Women Who Found Freedom. Akpaleeapik, Pond Inlet, Baffin Island.

Konjujuk's Friend. Told by Jermemiah Obed, Nain, Labrador. Also by Jørgen Skansen, Saqqaq, West Greenland.

Terqilik and His Sons. Cashier, Royal Greenland Trading Post, Angmagssalik, East Greenland.

Katiak. Collected from Ib Brodersen over a bottle of *imiak* (Greenland home brew). Angmagssalik, East Greenland.

Oherdluq, The Murderer. Gustav Broberg. Near Kulusuk, East Greenland.

Pavia, Who Made Friends With a Stone. Narrated by Anarfiik during a chat about ghosts. Sermiligaq, East Greenland.

Arnatsiq. Heard in Baffin Island and West Greenland.

The Jealous Husband. Angmagssalik, East Greenland.

Girl of Stone. Told by Nattiq while searching for seals in Rasmussen Basin, Northwest Territories.

The Woman Who Married Her Son's Wife. From Gustav Broberg. Kulusuk, East Greenland.

Tugtutsiak. Akpaleeapik, Pond Inlet, Baffin Island.

The Man Who Was a Mother. Told by an old man named Søren, concertina player extraordinaire. Igaliko, West Greenland.

Four Wives. Carver of *tupilaks,* who claimed to be a grandson of the murderer and his last wife. Kulusuk, East Greenland.

Nutik. Heard throughout the Arctic.

Mikisoq and the Skull. Collected in Saqqaq, West Greenland.

The Luckless Hunter. Pangnirtung, Baffin Island.

Nakasungnak, the Fool. Heard from a snowmachine repairman, Nuuq, West Greenland.

Two Men, One Kayak. Told by Ken Annanack, hiking through Auyuittuq National Park, Baffin Island.

Sermerssuaq. Told as a joke at a birthday party. Eskimo Point, Northwest Territories.

The Iron-Tailed Woman. From Ib Brodersen, Angmagssalik, East Greenland.

Asalok's Family. Versions heard in Greenland and Labrador.

Island of Women. Told by a man from Cape Dorset named Paulassie, who pointed out the "Island of Women" in Foxe Basin.

The Slab of Meat. Collected in Kulusuk, East Greenland.

V. ANIMALS

The Raven and the Seagull. Heard throughout the Arctic.

Whale's Wife. Told by Meqqoq. Sermiligaq, East Greenland.

The Mother's Skull. Collected from Anarfiik, Sermiligaq, East Greenland.

"Spare My Life". Inside a plastic igloo. Summer fishing encampment near Gjoa Haven, Northwest Territories.

The Raven and The Whale. Versions heard in Nain, Labrador; Pangnirtung, Baffin Island; and from a Danish mortician in Nuuq, West Greenland.

The Two Girls and their Husbands. Collected in Baffin Island and East Greenland.

Inugarssuk. Told by Anarfiik, Sermiligaq, East Greenland.

The Giant Eider Duck. Heard during a *kaffemik* ("coffee orgy"). Jakobshavn, West Greenland. Also told by a taxi driver in Frobisher Bay, Baffin Island.

The She-Bear. From Akpaleeapik's wife, Ukaleq ("Rabbit Woman"). Pond Inlet, Baffin Island.

The Wife Who Turned Into a Raven. Man feeding his dogs halibut heads. Near Cape Dorset, Baffin Island.

The Raven and the Hunter. Story told by Nattiq, who claimed to have heard it from a raven. Gjoa Haven, Northwest Territories.

The Eider Duck's Revenge. Man wearing a "Save the Eskimos" T-shirt. Eskimo Point, Northwest Territories.

"Am I Not a Handsome Brute?" Heard in Ummannaq, West Greenland.

The Greedy Eagle. Told by Paulassie. Cape Dorset, Baffin Island.

Guillemots. Versions collected in Labrador and West Greenland.

The Lustful Raven. Throughout the Arctic.

Tiggak. Told by Gustav Broberg after an unsuccessful seal hunt. Near Kulusuk, East Greenland.

VI. DEATH AND OLD AGE

The Collector of Ravens. Heard in Greenland and Baffin Island.

Meqqoq and the Stone People. Collected from Anarfiik and his wife. Sermiligaq, East Greenland.

The Magic Bear. Told by Ken Annanack, Pangnirtung, Baffin Island, at the anniversary party for the big wind which took away his home, the local nursing station, the community garage, and half the Hudson Bay Store.

The Kayaker Who Flew. Throughout the Arctic and Greenland.

The Old Woman Who Was Kind to Insects. Told by Jørgen Skansen, Saqqaq, West Greenland, during a plague of mosquitoes.

Natatoq, the Storyteller. From Ib Brodersen, who claimed to be a relation of Natatoq's. On a rock overlooking Angmagssalik Fjord.

The Hole in the Cliffs. Told by Nattiq. Near Gjoa Haven, Northwest Territories.

Old Age. Heard in Nain, Labrador, and East Greenland.

The Old Man Who Ate His Grandson. Based on an actual incident in the 1920s. Pond Inlet, Baffin Island.

Umaq, Who Danced. Man waiting for a bus. Nuuq, West Greenland.

Tuglik and Her Granddaughter. Heard from Anarfiik. Sermiligaq, East Greenland.

Neruvkak. Heard throughout the Arctic.

The Old Seal-Hunter from Aluk. Nanortalik, West Greenland.

"I Have Sent Them My Death..." Told by Elijah Saimat at the Grenfell Hospital, St. Anthony, Newfoundland.

The Man and His Wife Who Raised the Dead. Collected from Ib Brodersen over a meal of dried whale meat, potato chips, and *imiak* (Greenland home brew). Angmagssalik, East Greenland.

Skeletons. Told by Meqqoq. Sermiligaq, East Greenland.

Kivioq, Whose Kayak Was Full of Ghosts. Versions heard in Arctic Canada and both coasts of Greenland.

What is the Earth?. Throughout the Arctic and Greenland.